Building Wealth on the Internet

Jeremy Lopez

Building Wealth on the Internet

Published by Dr. Jeremy Lopez

Copyright © 2023

ENDORSEMENTS

Jeremy does an excellent job of giving balanced instruction on how to meditate, and also explaining the benefits that come from having a regular meditation and mindfulness practice. I love how Jeremy is not afraid to learn from and quote those outside the Christian tradition. He is able to explain the ancient concepts simply from a Biblical perspective. – Kari Browning, Director, *The Beautiful Revolution*

You are put on this earth with incredible potential and a divine destiny. This powerful, practical man shows you how to tap into power you did not even know you had. – Brian Tracy – Author, *The Power of Self Confidence*

I found myself savoring the concepts of the Law of Attraction merging with the Law of Creativity until slowly the beautiful truths seeped deeper into my thirsty soul. I am called to be a Creator! My friend, Dr. Jeremy Lopez, has a way of reminding us of our eternal 'I-Am-ness' while putting the tools in our hands to unlock our endless creative potential with the Divine mind. As a musical composer, I am excited to explore, with greater understanding, the infinite realm of possibilities as I place fingers on my piano and whisper, 'Let there be!' – Dony McGuire, Grammy Award winning artist and musical composer

Jeremy dives deep into the power of consciousness and shows us that we can create a world where the champion within us can shine and how we can manifest our desires to live a life of fulfillment. A must read! – Greg S. Reid – *Forbes* and *Inc.* top rated Keynote Speaker

I have been privileged to know Jeremy Lopez for many years, as well as sharing the platform with him at a number of conferences. Through this time, I have found him as a man of integrity, commitment, wisdom, and one of the most networked people I have met. Jeremy is an entrepreneur and a leader of leaders. He has amazing insights into leadership competencies and values. He has a passion to ignite this latent potential within individuals and organizations and provide ongoing development and coaching to bring about competitive advantage and success. I would highly recommend him as a speaker, coach, mentor, and consultant. – Chris Gaborit – Learning Leader, Trainer

Dr. Jeremy Lopez's book Universal Laws: Are They Biblical? is a breath of fresh air and much needed to answer the questions that people have been asking about the correlation between Biblical and Universal Laws. I have known Jeremy Lopez for years, and as a Biblical scholar, he gives an in-depth explanation and understanding of the perfect blending and merging into the secrets and mysteries of these miraculous Laws and how Bible-based the Universal Laws truly are. As the show host for the past twelve years on The Law of Attraction Radio Network, this book answers questions that I have received from Christian and spiritual seekers around the globe about the relationship between the metaphysical and Biblical truths. After reading this book, readers will feel empowered and have strong faith that God has indeed given us these Bible-based Universal and Divine Laws to tap into so that we can live and create an abundant life. – Constance Arnold, M.A., Author, Speaker, Professional Counselor, Host of *The Think, Believe & Manifest Talk Show*

TABLE OF CONTENTS

Preface

The world is larger than you think. In today's digital age, the internet has revolutionized the way we live, work, and interact with the world. One of the most significant advancements it has brought is the ability to generate income online. Whether you are looking for a side hustle or a full-time venture, the internet provides countless opportunities to earn money. It's time to explore various avenues for utilizing the internet to make money, ranging from freelance work to online businesses. Are you ready to finally make your dreams a reality?

Freelancing has become a popular choice for many individuals seeking flexible work arrangements and the opportunity to showcase their skills. Online platforms like Upwork, Freelancer, and Fiverr connect freelancers with clients worldwide. Whether you are a writer, graphic designer, programmer, or marketer, these platforms enable you to offer your services and find paid projects. By building a strong portfolio and establishing a reputation, you can attract more clients and increase your earning potential.

The rise of e-commerce has opened up new avenues for entrepreneurs to start their own online businesses. Platforms such as Shopify, Etsy, and Amazon provide a user-friendly interface to set up online stores and sell products to a global customer base. Additionally, dropshipping allows you to sell products without the need for inventory. You simply partner with suppliers who handle product storage and shipping on your behalf. With effective marketing strategies and customer-centric approach, e-commerce can be a lucrative venture.

Affiliate marketing is a performance-based model where you earn a commission by promoting other companies' products or services. You can join affiliate programs offered by various online retailers and promote their products through your website, blog, or social media channels. When someone makes a purchase using your referral link, you earn a percentage of the sale. Building a niche-focused website or establishing a strong social media presence can significantly increase your chances of success in affiliate marketing.

The demand for engaging and informative content is constantly growing, creating opportunities for individuals with creative skills. Whether it's writing blog posts, creating YouTube videos, or hosting podcasts, content creators can monetize their work through various channels. Platforms like YouTube, Twitch, and Patreon allow creators to earn money through ad revenue, sponsorships, donations, and subscriptions. By consistently delivering high-quality content and building a loyal audience, content creators can generate a substantial income.

The internet has made education accessible to people around the globe, and online learning platforms have gained immense popularity. If you possess expertise in a particular field, you can create and sell online courses. Platforms like Udemy, Teachable, and Coursera provide tools to create and market your courses to a wide audience. Additionally, coaching and consulting services have also gained traction. You can offer personalized coaching sessions, webinars, or group coaching programs, leveraging video conferencing tools like Zoom or Skype.

The internet has created an abundance of opportunities for individuals to make money online. Whether you choose to freelance, start an e-commerce business, engage in affiliate marketing, create content, or offer online courses, the key to success lies in dedication, continuous learning, and adaptability. As you explore these avenues, remember to focus on providing value to your audience or clients, building a strong online presence, and leveraging digital marketing techniques. With persistence and a proactive mindset, the internet can be a powerful tool for achieving financial independence and realizing your entrepreneurial dreams.

The rise of social media platforms has given birth to a new breed of influencers who have turned their online presence into a profitable business. Influencer marketing has become a popular avenue for brands to reach their target audience.

If you have a significant following on platforms like Instagram, TikTok, or YouTube, you can collaborate with brands and promote their products or services. Brands may offer sponsored content, affiliate partnerships, or brand ambassadorships, providing you with an opportunity to monetize your influence. Building an authentic and engaged community is crucial for long-term success in this field.

While not as lucrative as some other methods, participating in online surveys and market research can still provide a modest source of income. Many companies and research firms rely on consumer opinions to improve their products or services. Websites like Swagbucks, Survey Junkie, and Toluna offer paid surveys, product testing, and online focus groups. While the income potential may vary, it can be a simple way to make some extra money during your free time.

As businesses and entrepreneurs navigate the digital landscape, the demand for virtual assistants has grown substantially. Virtual assistants provide administrative, creative, or technical support remotely. Tasks may include managing emails, scheduling appointments, social media management, content creation, or data entry. Platforms like Upwork and Freelancer connect virtual assistants with clients in need of their services. By honing your organizational and communication skills, you can build a successful virtual assistant business.

With the rise of cryptocurrencies like Bitcoin and Ethereum, individuals have found opportunities to generate income through online trading. Cryptocurrency trading involves buying and selling digital currencies on exchanges to take advantage of price fluctuations. It requires knowledge of market trends, analysis, and risk management. Additionally, online trading platforms offer opportunities to trade stocks, commodities, and forex. While trading can be lucrative, it also carries risks, so thorough research, education, and caution are essential.

Investing in online real estate has gained popularity with the growth of the internet. Buying and selling domain names or websites can be a profitable venture. You can identify valuable domain names or websites, acquire them, and sell them at a higher price. Similarly, investing in online properties like blogs or niche websites with a steady traffic flow can provide passive income through advertising or affiliate marketing. Additionally, platforms like Airbnb allow property owners to rent out their spaces to travelers, providing an opportunity for extra income.

The internet has transformed the way we conduct business and has opened up an array of opportunities for generating income. From leveraging social media influence to trading cryptocurrencies, the online world offers diverse avenues to explore. As with any venture, it is important to conduct thorough research, continuously learn and adapt, and focus on providing value to your target audience or clients. By harnessing the power of the internet, you can create a sustainable and fulfilling income stream while enjoying the flexibility and potential for growth that the online world provides.

In a world where financial stability and abundance are often seen as distant dreams, it is crucial to recognize and affirm your own worthiness of achieving financial freedom and wealth. This chapter aims to empower and motivate you by highlighting the reasons why you truly deserve to embrace financial abundance in your life.

You are inherently deserving of financial freedom and wealth simply because you are a valuable human being. Your worth is not determined by your past financial circumstances or current situation. Regardless of your background or previous experiences, you have unique skills, talents, and potential that can contribute to your own success and the well-being of others. Embrace the understanding that you have something valuable to offer to the world.

You deserve financial freedom because you have the power to shape your own destiny. By cultivating a positive mindset, setting clear goals, and taking consistent action, you can create a life of abundance and fulfillment. Recognize that you have the ability to make choices and decisions that will lead you towards financial independence. Embrace the responsibility of actively designing your financial future.

Financial freedom and wealth can enable you to make a positive impact on the world around you. When you have the means to support yourself and your loved ones, you can also extend that support to causes and organizations that align with your values. By becoming financially secure, you can contribute to charitable endeavors, support local businesses, create job opportunities, and invest in initiatives that improve society as a whole. Recognize the potential you have to make a difference and the importance of your financial success in achieving that.

Embracing financial freedom and wealth is a testament to your commitment to personal growth and self-care. By prioritizing your financial well-being, you can ensure stability and security in your life. This stability creates a solid foundation upon which you can pursue personal and professional growth, explore your passions, and invest in your own development. Financial freedom affords you the time and resources to prioritize self-care and nurture your physical, mental, and emotional well-being. You deserve the opportunity to live a fulfilling and abundant life.

Another reason why you deserve financial freedom and wealth is your desire to provide for your loved ones. Whether it's supporting your family, ensuring your children's education, or creating opportunities for your loved ones, financial abundance allows you to nurture and care for those dear to you. You deserve to experience the joy of providing security, comfort, and opportunities for your family and loved ones.

Financial freedom and wealth are not exclusive privileges reserved for a select few. You deserve to embrace abundance and prosperity in your life. Recognize your inherent value, take control of your destiny, and acknowledge the positive impact you can make on the world. Prioritize personal growth, self-care, and the well-being of your loved ones. Remember that you are deserving of financial freedom, and with dedication, perseverance, and a positive mindset, you can manifest the abundance you truly deserve.

Introduction

On a memorable episode of the Today show, iconic hosts Katie Couric and Bryant Gumbel engaged in a fascinating discussion about the internet. This historic moment took place on January 24, 1994, during a time when the internet was still a relatively new and unfamiliar concept to many people.

During the segment, Couric and Gumbel tried to make sense of this emerging technology, showcasing their curiosity and sometimes humorous confusion. The clip of their conversation has since become a viral sensation, highlighting the early skepticism and confusion surrounding the internet's potential impact on society.

At the beginning of the segment, Couric posed a fundamental question, asking Gumbel, "What is the internet, anyway?" This innocent query reflected the general uncertainty that prevailed during that time, with many struggling to grasp the concept and the significance of this global network of interconnected computers.

Gumbel responded by humorously admitting that he didn't know much about the internet, referring to it as a "series of tubes" and suggesting that it was something that was "not a big truck." His analogy, although incorrect, illustrated the difficulty in understanding a complex and intangible technology like the internet.

The conversation continued as they delved into various aspects of the internet. Couric inquired about email and its relevance, to which Gumbel admitted he was still a fan of traditional mail and was unsure about the need for electronic messages. They also discussed the term "@," which was commonly used in email addresses, and its perplexing meaning.

Throughout the segment, Couric and Gumbel maintained an open and inquisitive attitude, showcasing the willingness to learn and explore this new digital landscape. Their genuine curiosity and candid reactions resonated with viewers and helped to humanize the confusion surrounding the internet's emergence.

Little did they know at the time that their discussion would become an enduring moment in broadcast history. The clip resurfaced years later, gaining traction on the internet itself, and became a symbol of the early stages of digital transformation. It served as a reminder of how far technology had come and the rapid evolution of our connected world.

Katie Couric and Bryant Gumbel's conversation on the Today show exemplified the era when the internet was still a mystery to many, highlighting the challenges and curiosity associated with this transformative technology. Their genuine and relatable exchange resonated with audiences then and continues to capture the essence of that pivotal time in our technological history.

As the years went by, the internet grew and evolved at an astonishing pace, surpassing the expectations of even the most visionary individuals. The viral clip of Katie Couric and Bryant Gumbel discussing the internet became a time capsule, representing a moment when the world was just beginning to comprehend the immense potential of this digital revolution.

In subsequent episodes of the Today show, Couric and Gumbel revisited the topic of the internet, embracing its significance and embracing the opportunities it presented. They interviewed experts, explored emerging technologies, and highlighted the ways in which the internet was transforming various aspects of society, including communication, commerce, and entertainment.

Over time, Couric and Gumbel themselves became tech-savvy hosts, adapting to the ever-changing digital landscape. They recognized the internet's ability to connect people, bridge distances, and disseminate information in ways that were previously unimaginable. Their continued coverage of internet-related topics reflected the growing understanding and acceptance of this powerful tool.

Fast forward to the present day, and the internet has become an integral part of our lives. It has revolutionized industries, disrupted traditional business models, and transformed the way we communicate, learn, and entertain ourselves. The once-perplexing concept of the internet has become so ingrained in our daily routines that we can scarcely imagine a world without it.

Katie Couric and Bryant Gumbel's discussion about the internet on the Today show stands as a testament to the early stages of this transformative technology. It serves as a reminder of the humble beginnings and the collective journey we have taken to integrate the internet into every aspect of our lives.

As we reflect on that historic episode, we recognize the importance of embracing new technologies, even when they seem daunting or confusing at first. It is a reminder to approach the ever-evolving digital landscape with an open mind and a willingness to adapt.

The Today show episode featuring Katie Couric and Bryant Gumbel discussing the internet became an iconic moment that captured the early curiosity, skepticism, and eventual acceptance of this groundbreaking technology. Their genuine exploration and subsequent embrace of the internet showcased the human capacity to adapt and grow, serving as a timeless reminder of the transformative power of innovation.

The internet has undergone a remarkable transformation since its inception. From its humble beginnings as a network connecting a few computers to a global phenomenon that permeates almost every aspect of our lives, the internet has truly revolutionized the way we communicate, access information, conduct business, and interact with the world. In this chapter, we will explore the remarkable journey of the internet, from its early days to the cutting-edge technologies that have propelled it into the digital frontier.

The internet's story begins in the 1960s, during the Cold War era, when the United States Department of Defense initiated a research project known as ARPANET. The goal was to develop a decentralized communication network that could withstand a nuclear attack. In 1969, the first message was sent over ARPANET, marking the birth of the internet. Initially, it connected only a handful of computers at research institutions, but its potential for information exchange was clear.

In 1989, a significant milestone in the internet's evolution occurred when Tim Berners-Lee, a British computer scientist, invented the World Wide Web. Berners-Lee's creation introduced a user-friendly interface for navigating the internet using hypertext links. The web made it possible to access and share information through webpages, which led to an exponential growth of content and the rapid expansion of the internet's user base.

The 1990s witnessed the advent of the commercial internet and the dot-com boom. As more businesses and entrepreneurs recognized the internet's potential, countless startups emerged, fueled by venture capital investments.

E-commerce sites, such as Amazon and eBay, disrupted traditional retail models. Internet giants like Yahoo!, Google, and AOL revolutionized search and content discovery. The dot-com bubble eventually burst in the early 2000s, but it laid the foundation for the internet's future growth and innovation.

In the early days of the internet, most users accessed it via dial-up connections, which were slow and limited in bandwidth. However, the widespread adoption of broadband internet in the late 1990s and early 2000s transformed the internet experience. Broadband provided high-speed connectivity, enabling faster downloads, streaming media, and richer online experiences. As technology advanced, broadband evolved from Digital Subscriber Line (DSL) to cable, fiber optics, and wireless connections, empowering users with faster and more reliable internet access.

The 2000s marked the emergence of social media platforms that transformed the way we connect and share information online. Websites like Friendster, MySpace, and Facebook enabled users to create profiles, connect with friends, and share photos and updates. YouTube revolutionized video-sharing, while Twitter introduced the concept of microblogging. Social media's impact on society, politics, and culture cannot be overstated, as it became a powerful tool for communication, activism, and influence.

The internet's reach expanded exponentially with the advent of mobile devices, particularly smartphones. The launch of the iPhone in 2007 revolutionized the mobile industry and brought the internet to people's pockets. Mobile internet usage soared as smartphones became more affordable and accessible, allowing users to access the internet anytime, anywhere. Mobile apps further enhanced the internet experience, offering a wide range of services, from entertainment and productivity to health and education.

The Internet of Things (IoT) represents a new phase in the internet's evolution, where everyday objects are embedded with sensors, software, and connectivity, allowing them to collect and exchange data. This interconnected network of devices has opened up a world of possibilities, enabling seamless automation, data-driven decision-making, and improved efficiency across various sectors. Smart homes equipped with IoT devices can regulate temperature, monitor security, and control appliances remotely. In healthcare, IoT devices like wearable fitness trackers and remote patient monitoring systems have revolutionized personal health management. Industries such as manufacturing, agriculture, and transportation have embraced

IoT solutions to optimize operations, reduce costs, and enhance productivity.

Cloud computing has revolutionized the way we store, access, and process data over the internet. Rather than relying on local servers, individuals and businesses can now store their data in remote servers, accessed through the internet. Cloud computing offers scalability, cost-efficiency, and easy collaboration, enabling businesses to focus on their core competencies while leveraging powerful computing resources. Moreover, the proliferation of data generated by various online activities, IoT devices, and social media has given rise to the concept of big data. Advanced analytics tools and machine learning algorithms can process and derive insights from massive datasets, leading to improved decision-making, personalized experiences, and targeted marketing.

The internet has come a long way since its inception, evolving into a global network that has transformed nearly every aspect of our lives. From its humble beginnings as a defense project to the digital frontier of today, the internet has connected people across continents, democratized information access, and catalyzed innovation on an unprecedented scale. As we continue to push the boundaries of technology, it is essential to navigate the internet's evolution responsibly, addressing challenges and ensuring that it remains a force for good, enabling connectivity, knowledge sharing, and positive societal impact.

The internet has opened up countless opportunities for individuals to leverage their skills, creativity, and entrepreneurial spirit to make money online. Whether you're looking to generate a side income or build a full-fledged online business, the internet provides a wealth of avenues to explore. In this chapter, we will delve into various strategies and platforms that can help you utilize the internet to your advantage and generate income.

One of the most popular ways to make money on the internet is through e-commerce. Platforms like Amazon, eBay, and Etsy offer individuals the opportunity to sell products online. You can either create your own unique products or leverage dropshipping, where you partner with suppliers to sell their products without holding inventory. Building an online store or utilizing existing marketplaces allows you to reach a global audience, providing the potential for significant sales and profits.

The internet has revolutionized the way people work, opening up a vast array of freelancing and remote work opportunities. Websites like Upwork, Freelancer, and Fiverr connect freelancers with clients seeking their skills, whether it's writing, graphic design, programming, marketing, or consulting. Remote work platforms like Remote.co and FlexJobs enable individuals to find full-time or part-time remote positions across various industries. Freelancing and remote work offer flexibility, independence, and the potential to earn a substantial income.

The rise of digital content consumption has created opportunities for individuals to monetize their creativity and expertise. Starting a blog, vlog (video blog), or podcast allows you to share valuable content and build an audience. You can monetize your content through advertising, sponsored content, affiliate marketing, or by offering premium subscriptions or digital products. Platforms like YouTube, Twitch, and Patreon provide avenues for content creators to earn money through ads, sponsorships, donations, or memberships.

The internet has democratized education, allowing individuals to create and sell online courses, webinars, and tutorials. If you have expertise in a particular field, you can package your knowledge into a comprehensive course and sell it on platforms like Udemy, Coursera, Teachable, or your own website. Online courses offer the advantage of scalability, as you can reach a large audience and generate passive income. Additionally, you can offer coaching or consulting services to provide personalized guidance and support.

Affiliate marketing involves promoting products or services on your website, blog, or social media platforms and earning a commission for each sale or lead generated through your referral. By joining affiliate programs offered by companies such as Amazon, Commission Junction, or ShareASale, you can select products relevant to your audience and earn a commission for successful conversions. Building a strong online presence and strategically promoting affiliate products can lead to substantial income over time.

The internet has also provided opportunities for individuals to engage in online investing and trading. Stock trading platforms like Robinhood, E*TRADE, and TD Ameritrade allow individuals to buy and sell stocks, bonds, and other financial instruments with ease. Additionally, cryptocurrency trading has gained significant popularity, with platforms like Coinbase and Binance enabling users to trade digital currencies. However, it's important to approach investing and trading with caution, conducting thorough research and understanding the associated risks.

The rise of social media has given birth to a new breed of influencers who can leverage their online presence to collaborate with brands and earn money. Influencers with a sizable following on platforms like Instagram, TikTok, or YouTube can partner with brands for sponsored content, product endorsements, or brand ambassadorships.

The Internet Has a Job

In the vast landscape of technology and information exchange, the Internet stands as a powerful and indispensable entity. Its existence is not arbitrary or haphazard; instead, the Internet has a very specific job to do. It serves as a global network that connects billions of devices, people, and systems, facilitating communication, information sharing, and countless other services. This chapter explores the fundamental purpose of the Internet and how it fulfills its specific job in today's interconnected world.

The Internet's primary task is to serve as the information superhighway, an intricate network of interconnected devices that enables the flow of data across the globe. It provides a means for individuals, businesses, governments, and organizations to transmit, access, and exchange information in various forms, such as text, images, audio, and video. This capability has revolutionized how we communicate, learn, conduct business, and navigate the modern world.

One of the Internet's essential functions is to facilitate communication between people regardless of their geographical location. Through email, instant messaging, voice and video calls, and social media platforms, individuals can connect with one another in real-time, transcending borders and time zones. The Internet has transformed the way we interact, fostering global communities, and enabling collaborations on an unprecedented scale.

The Internet's role as an information-sharing platform cannot be overstated. It serves as an immense repository of knowledge, where individuals can publish and access information on virtually any topic. Websites, blogs, online forums, and educational platforms have democratized the availability of information, empowering people with instant access to a wealth of resources. Whether it's seeking answers, conducting research, or staying informed, the Internet has become an indispensable tool for acquiring knowledge.

Another crucial aspect of the Internet's job is facilitating electronic commerce (e-commerce) and digital transactions. Online marketplaces, such as Amazon and eBay, allow businesses and individuals to buy and sell products and services across the globe. The Internet provides a secure platform for online payments, ensuring the safe transfer of funds. Moreover, digital currencies and blockchain technology have emerged, further revolutionizing financial transactions and opening new avenues for economic growth and innovation.

The Internet has transformed the entertainment and media landscape, making it easier for creators to share their work with the world. Platforms like YouTube, Netflix, and Spotify provide access to a vast array of multimedia content, including videos, movies, music, and podcasts. Streaming services have disrupted traditional broadcasting, giving consumers more control over what, when, and how they consume media. The Internet's specific job in this context is to serve as a conduit for entertainment and media consumption, enriching our lives with diverse content and experiences.

In recent years, the Internet's job has extended beyond connecting people to connecting devices, giving rise to the Internet of Things (IoT). IoT enables the interconnectivity of everyday objects and systems, allowing them to collect and exchange data. From smart homes to industrial automation, the Internet plays a pivotal role in enabling intelligent devices and automation, revolutionizing sectors such as healthcare, transportation, and manufacturing.

The Internet's specific job is to serve as a global network that connects devices, people, and systems, empowering communication, information sharing, and numerous other services. From facilitating global communication and information access to revolutionizing commerce, entertainment, and automation, the Internet has become an essential component of our daily lives. As technology continues to evolve, the Internet will undoubtedly adapt and refine its job to meet the changing needs of our increasingly interconnected world.

As the Internet's role in our lives expands, so does the importance of ensuring secure and private communication. The Internet has a specific job of providing mechanisms and technologies to safeguard sensitive information and protect users' privacy. Encryption protocols, secure browsing, and virtual private networks (VPNs) are just a few examples of the tools available to safeguard our digital interactions. The Internet's ability to fulfill its specific job relies on creating an environment of trust, where individuals can confidently engage in online activities while maintaining their privacy and security.

The Internet serves as a catalyst for collaboration and innovation, bringing together diverse perspectives and expertise from around the world. Platforms like GitHub and GitLab enable developers to collaborate on open-source projects, accelerating software development and fostering a culture of knowledge sharing. Crowdsourcing platforms allow individuals to contribute to scientific research, design projects, and social initiatives. The Internet's specific job is to empower individuals and organizations to collaborate, share ideas, and drive innovation, ultimately advancing human progress in various fields.

The Internet has become a powerful tool for activism and social change, amplifying voices that might otherwise go unheard. Social media platforms, online petitions, and digital campaigns enable individuals to raise awareness about important issues and mobilize support for causes they believe in. The Internet's specific job in this context is to break down barriers, connect like-minded individuals, and provide a platform for advocacy, ultimately driving societal transformation and promoting social justice.

The COVID-19 pandemic showcased the Internet's crucial role in enabling remote work and education. As millions of people transitioned to remote setups, the Internet became the backbone of virtual meetings, collaboration tools, and online learning platforms. The Internet's specific job expanded to ensure seamless connectivity, enabling individuals to work, learn, and connect remotely. This shift in the way we work and educate ourselves has the potential to redefine traditional systems, making knowledge and job opportunities more accessible and flexible.

The Internet's specific job is not fixed but rather evolves in response to societal needs and technological advancements. As new technologies emerge, such as 5G networks, artificial intelligence (AI), and virtual reality (VR), the Internet will continue to adapt and expand its capabilities. The Internet's job will encompass more immersive experiences, intelligent automation, and enhanced connectivity, pushing the boundaries of what is possible in the digital realm.

The Internet's specific job is multi-faceted and constantly evolving. From connecting devices and people to facilitating communication, information sharing, commerce, and entertainment, the Internet has become an indispensable part of our lives. Its role in promoting collaboration, empowering activism, securing communication, and enabling remote work and education cannot be overlooked. As we move forward, the Internet will undoubtedly continue to evolve, shaping the future of human interaction, innovation, and progress.

In a world characterized by diversity, geographical distances, and cultural differences, the Internet stands as a unifying force, bringing people from all walks of life together. This chapter explores how the Internet transcends barriers and bridges divides, fostering global connectivity, understanding, and collaboration. Through its expansive reach and accessibility, the Internet has revolutionized the way we interact, share information, and build relationships, ultimately creating a more interconnected and inclusive world.

One of the Internet's most profound impacts is its ability to connect individuals across borders, enabling communication and fostering global friendships. Through social media platforms, messaging apps, and online communities, people can engage in real-time conversations, share experiences, and build relationships with others from different countries and cultures. The Internet provides a platform for cultural exchange, breaking down traditional barriers and promoting a sense of global community.

The Internet has become a virtual melting pot of diverse cultures, ideas, and perspectives. Websites, blogs, and social media platforms serve as channels for sharing stories, traditions, and artistic expressions from around the world.

Through these digital platforms, we gain insights into different cultures, fostering empathy, understanding, and appreciation for our shared humanity. The Internet has played a vital role in promoting cultural exchange and breaking down stereotypes, allowing us to celebrate the richness and diversity of global cultures.

The Internet has transformed collaboration, allowing individuals and organizations to work together irrespective of their physical locations. Online project management tools, virtual meetings, and cloud-based platforms enable seamless collaboration on a global scale. Whether it's a team of researchers from different continents working on a groundbreaking discovery or individuals with shared passions forming international communities, the Internet brings people together, fostering collaboration and innovation across boundaries.

The Internet has played a significant role in giving a voice to marginalized communities and amplifying their stories. Social media campaigns, online petitions, and digital activism have empowered individuals and groups to raise awareness about social justice issues and advocate for change. Through online platforms, marginalized communities have found solidarity, support, and the ability to challenge oppressive systems. The Internet's ability to connect and mobilize has facilitated movements for equality, human rights, and social inclusion.

The Internet has revolutionized education and knowledge sharing, making information more accessible and leveling the playing field for learners worldwide. Online courses, educational platforms, and open educational resources have expanded learning opportunities, allowing individuals to access quality education regardless of their location or socio-economic background.

The Internet serves as a gateway to vast repositories of knowledge, empowering self-directed learning and enabling individuals to acquire new skills and expertise.

The Internet has transformed the global marketplace, enabling businesses of all sizes to engage in international trade and expand their reach. E-commerce platforms, online marketplaces, and digital payment systems have facilitated seamless transactions and eliminated geographical barriers. Small businesses and entrepreneurs can now compete on a global scale, connecting with customers and suppliers worldwide. The Internet has created opportunities for economic growth and empowerment, fostering a more interconnected global economy.

The Internet serves as a powerful bridge that connects people across borders, cultures, and backgrounds. Through its ability to transcend geographical distances, the Internet fosters cultural exchange, collaboration, and understanding. It empowers marginalized communities, democratizes education, and facilitates global trade and commerce. As we continue to leverage the Internet's potential, we must ensure its accessibility, inclusivity, and responsible use, allowing it to truly bring us all together and create a more connected and harmonious world.

In the vast realm of technological advancements, the Internet has emerged as one of the most valuable tools in existence. Its impact spans across various domains, transforming the way we live, work, communicate, and access information. This chapter explores the immense value of the Internet, highlighting its pivotal role in empowering individuals, driving innovation, and shaping the modern world. From connecting people globally to revolutionizing industries, the Internet's significance cannot be overstated.

The Internet has empowered individuals in unprecedented ways. It has democratized access to information, enabling individuals to educate themselves, explore new ideas, and expand their horizons. Online platforms offer opportunities for self-expression, creativity, and entrepreneurship, allowing individuals to share their knowledge, skills, and talents with the world. Moreover, the Internet has given a voice to marginalized communities, providing a platform to advocate for their rights and amplify their stories. By granting individuals the power to connect, learn, and contribute, the Internet has transformed the way we engage with the world and pursue our aspirations.

Innovation thrives in an environment that encourages collaboration, knowledge sharing, and rapid information exchange. The Internet has become a catalyst for innovation, connecting minds from diverse backgrounds and facilitating collaboration on a global scale. Through open-source communities, online forums, and virtual workspaces, individuals and organizations can collaborate and share ideas effortlessly. The Internet's vast repository of information and resources serves as a wellspring for inspiration and problem-solving, propelling scientific discoveries, technological advancements, and creative breakthroughs. It has shortened the innovation cycle, accelerating progress across numerous fields, from medicine and engineering to art and entertainment.

The Internet has disrupted and revolutionized traditional industries, ushering in a new era of digital transformation. E-commerce platforms have transformed the retail landscape, providing convenience and global access to products and services. Online streaming services have reshaped the entertainment industry, allowing consumers to access a vast array of multimedia content anytime, anywhere. The Internet of Things (IoT) has revolutionized manufacturing, transportation, and healthcare by connecting devices and enabling data-driven decision-making. The Internet's impact on industries has not only improved efficiency and productivity but has also opened up new avenues for economic growth and job creation.

At its core, the Internet is a communication tool that connects people across the globe. It has transformed the way we communicate, enabling instant, real-time interactions regardless of geographical distance. Social media platforms, messaging apps, and video conferencing tools have brought friends, families, and colleagues closer, fostering global connections and nurturing relationships. The Internet has transcended barriers of time and space, making the world more interconnected and accessible. It has become a lifeline during times of crisis, facilitating communication, and providing vital information to affected communities.

Collaboration has always been a driving force behind human progress, and the Internet has taken collaboration to new heights. It enables global collaboration by connecting individuals, teams, and organizations across borders. Remote work and virtual teams have become the norm, allowing professionals to collaborate seamlessly despite being geographically dispersed. International research collaborations have led to groundbreaking discoveries and advancements. The Internet's ability to facilitate global collaboration has accelerated innovation, fostered cross-cultural understanding, and enabled collective problem-solving on a scale never seen before.

The Internet stands as one of the most invaluable tools in existence, empowering individuals, driving innovation, and transforming industries. Its impact reaches far and wide, revolutionizing the way we live, work, communicate, and access information. By connecting people globally, accelerating innovation, and enhancing collaboration, the Internet has become an indispensable asset in our daily lives. As we navigate the ever-evolving digital landscape, it is important to recognize the responsibility that comes with harnessing the power of the Internet. Safeguarding privacy, promoting digital literacy, and ensuring equal access to its benefits are crucial considerations.

The Internet's value extends beyond its technical infrastructure; it lies in its ability to empower individuals, foster creativity, and drive positive change. As we move forward, it is essential to continue exploring the untapped potential of the

Internet while addressing its challenges. Ensuring a secure and inclusive digital ecosystem will enable us to fully leverage the Internet's value and harness its transformative power for the betterment of society.

The Internet's value as one of the most invaluable tools in existence cannot be overstated. It has revolutionized how we connect, collaborate, and access information. From empowering individuals and driving innovation to transforming industries and enhancing communication, the Internet has reshaped the modern world. However, with its vast potential comes the need for responsible and ethical use. By embracing the Internet's power while actively addressing its challenges, we can continue to unlock its immense value and create a more connected, informed, and inclusive global community.

"Keywords"

In the vast landscape of the internet, search engines act as gateways to information. They allow users to explore the digital realm by retrieving relevant web pages based on their queries. Behind the scenes, search engines employ various algorithms and techniques to match user intent with web content. One of the fundamental elements in this process is the use of keywords. In this chapter, we will delve into the role of keywords in search engines, exploring their importance, how search engines interpret and rank them, and the evolution of keyword usage over time.

Keywords are words or phrases that capture the essence of a topic, concept, or user query. They act as signals for search engines to identify and index relevant web pages. When a user enters a query into a search engine, the search engine analyzes the keywords in the query to provide the most appropriate results. Search engines also use keywords to determine the relevance of web pages to specific queries, helping them rank pages based on their perceived quality and usefulness.

Keywords play a vital role in search engines, enabling them to deliver accurate and relevant results to users. By understanding the keywords in a query, search engines can determine user intent and match it with web content that satisfies that intent. Effective use of keywords helps search engines improve user satisfaction and retention, as users are more likely to find the information they seek.

To comprehend the meaning and context of keywords, search engines employ sophisticated algorithms and natural language processing techniques. These algorithms analyze not only the individual words but also their relationships and semantic connections. By understanding the intent behind a keyword, search engines can provide results that are more relevant to the user's query.

Search engines use various strategies to interpret and index keywords effectively. One approach is stemming, where search engines reduce words to their base form to capture a broader range of related terms. For example, a search for "running shoes" may also return results for "run" or "runner." Another technique is the use of synonyms and related terms, allowing search engines to understand the context of a query beyond the explicit keywords used.

Once search engines understand the keywords in a query, they must determine the relevance and ranking of web pages. Numerous factors influence this process, including the presence and placement of keywords on a webpage, the authority and reputation of the website, and user engagement metrics.

Keyword placement is crucial for search engine optimization (SEO). Search engines typically prioritize keywords in certain locations, such as the page title, headings, meta tags, and the body of the content. When keywords appear in these areas, search engines consider the webpage more relevant to the query and rank it higher in the search results.

Over time, search engines have evolved in their understanding and utilization of keywords. Initially, search engines heavily relied on exact keyword matching. Webmasters optimized their content by strategically repeating keywords to rank higher in search results. However, this approach led to poor user experiences, as content quality and relevance were often sacrificed for keyword density.

In response, search engines have become more sophisticated in their algorithms. They now consider the overall context of the webpage, the user's search history, and user engagement signals to determine relevance. The focus has shifted from exact keyword matching to understanding user intent and providing high-quality content that satisfies that intent.

Furthermore, advancements in natural language processing and machine learning have allowed search engines to grasp the meaning behind search queries more accurately. This enables them to provide more relevant results even when the keywords used may not precisely match the content on a webpage.

Keywords are essential components of search engine functionality. They allow search engines to understand user queries, interpret the context, and deliver relevant results. The proper use of keywords is crucial for both users and website owners. Users can improve their search experience by using relevant keywords that accurately reflect their intent. On the other hand, website owners and content creators need to optimize their web pages by incorporating relevant keywords strategically.

To ensure the effective use of keywords, it is important to conduct keyword research. This process involves identifying the most relevant and commonly searched keywords related to a specific topic or industry. Keyword research tools, such as Google Keyword Planner, can provide valuable insights into search volume, competition, and related keywords. By incorporating these researched keywords into their content, website owners increase the visibility of their pages in search engine results.

However, it's important to note that search engines have become more sophisticated in their approach to keywords. They no longer solely rely on exact keyword matching, but also consider the overall context, user intent, and content quality. This shift is aimed at providing users with the most relevant and high-quality content that aligns with their search queries.

Keyword stuffing, which refers to the excessive and irrelevant use of keywords, is strongly discouraged by search engines. It can lead to penalties, where search engines may lower the ranking of a webpage or even remove it from search results altogether. Instead, website owners should focus on creating valuable, informative, and engaging content that naturally incorporates relevant keywords.

In recent years, search engines have also started to understand user queries beyond just keywords. They have embraced natural language processing and artificial intelligence to comprehend the intent behind a query and deliver more accurate results. This evolution has been driven by the increasing use of voice search and conversational queries, where users tend to phrase their queries as complete questions or sentences rather than just keywords.

As search engines continue to evolve, the use of keywords will remain a crucial aspect of optimizing web content. However, website owners and content creators should prioritize user experience, relevance, and content quality over keyword density. By focusing on providing valuable information that satisfies user intent, they can ensure that their web pages rank higher in search engine results and attract organic traffic.

Keywords play a significant role in search engine functionality, helping search engines understand user intent and deliver relevant results. However, the approach to keywords has shifted from exact matching to understanding context and user intent. Website owners and content creators should conduct keyword research, incorporate relevant keywords naturally into their content, and prioritize content quality and user experience to optimize their web pages for search engines. By staying up-to-date with the latest developments in search engine algorithms, they can adapt their keyword strategies to provide the best possible experience for both users and search engines.

The continuous advancement of search engine technology has brought about several new developments and trends in how keywords are used. Let's explore some of these trends:

Long-Tail Keywords: Long-tail keywords are longer, more specific phrases that target niche topics or user queries. As search engines become better at understanding user intent, there is a growing emphasis on long-tail keywords. These keywords tend to have lower search volume but higher conversion rates, as they cater to users with specific needs or interests. For example, instead of targeting the broad keyword "running shoes," a long-tail keyword could be "best trail running shoes for flat feet." By optimizing content for long-tail keywords, website owners can attract highly targeted traffic and improve their chances of conversion.

Semantic Search: Semantic search focuses on understanding the context and meaning behind a user's query, rather than relying solely on specific keywords. Search engines now consider related concepts, synonyms, and the overall context of the query to deliver more accurate results. This approach allows search engines to provide more relevant content, even if it doesn't contain the exact keywords used in the search query. Website owners should consider incorporating related terms and concepts into their content to align with semantic search and improve their visibility in search results.

Voice Search Optimization: With the rise of voice assistants and smart devices, voice search has become increasingly popular. Voice queries tend to be more conversational and longer, mimicking natural language. As a result, website owners need to optimize their content for voice search by considering the way people speak and phrase their queries. This includes using more natural language, targeting question-based queries, and providing concise and direct answers to commonly asked questions. Voice search optimization requires a deeper understanding of user intent and how people interact with search engines using voice commands.

User Experience Signals: Search engines are placing greater emphasis on user experience signals when ranking web pages. Factors such as page load speed, mobile responsiveness, user engagement, and overall website usability now influence search engine rankings. While keywords remain important, search engines consider the overall user experience as a measure of content quality and relevance. Website owners should prioritize providing a seamless and engaging user experience to enhance their search engine visibility and improve their chances of ranking higher in search results.

Personalized Search: Search engines are personalizing search results based on individual user preferences, location, search history, and behavior. Personalized search aims to deliver more relevant and tailored results to each user. This means that search rankings can vary from person to person, even for the same keyword. Website owners should focus on creating high-quality content that resonates with their target audience and engages users consistently. By understanding their audience and delivering personalized experiences, website owners can improve their chances of appearing in personalized search results.

The landscape of keyword usage in search engines continues to evolve. Website owners and content creators need to adapt their keyword strategies to align with these trends. By incorporating long-tail keywords, understanding semantic search, optimizing for voice search, prioritizing user experience, and considering personalized search, website owners can improve their visibility and drive more relevant organic traffic to their web pages. Keeping up with the latest developments in search engine technology and staying proactive in keyword research and optimization will be crucial for success in the ever-changing world of search engines.

So, by now you must be wondering, "Jeremy, what does this have to do with making money?" Well, quite literally everything. Knowing how the internet works, you become more able to use it to your advantage. It's time to start putting the internet to work for you. Are you ready?

Finding Your Story

As the sun dipped below the horizon, casting a golden glow across the city, Sarah couldn't help but reflect on the incredible journey that had brought her to this moment. Her life had been a tapestry woven with diverse experiences, both triumphs, and tribulations. Little did she know that the stories she carried within her would become the foundation for an extraordinary business empire.

Sarah had always possessed a unique ability to connect with people on a profound level. From a young age, she found solace in the pages of books, devouring tales of human resilience and the power of personal narratives. Through the struggles and triumphs of others, she discovered the strength to face her own challenges head-on.

After years of personal growth and self-discovery, Sarah had amassed a treasure trove of stories—her own and those she had encountered along the way. She realized that these stories held immense value, not just for herself but for others as well. They were the keys to unlocking empathy, inspiration, and personal transformation.

With a newfound purpose burning in her heart, Sarah set out to share these stories with the world. She started by creating a blog where she poured her heart out, sharing her experiences, insights, and the lessons she had learned. The response was overwhelming. People resonated with her vulnerability, and they began to share their own stories, finding solace and support in the virtual community she had created.

But Sarah's ambitions went beyond a mere blog. She recognized the potential to turn her passion into a thriving business. With her unwavering determination and entrepreneurial spirit, she began to explore different avenues for monetizing her storytelling skills.

First, Sarah compiled her most compelling stories into a captivating memoir. The book struck a chord with readers worldwide, becoming an instant bestseller. Its success catapulted Sarah into the spotlight, where she became a sought-after speaker at conferences and events. Her ability to captivate audiences with her storytelling prowess led to numerous lucrative speaking engagements.

As Sarah's influence grew, so did her ambition. She saw an opportunity to create a platform that could amplify the power of storytelling even further. Drawing from her own experiences and the stories she had collected over the years, she developed an online course that taught individuals how to harness the transformative power of storytelling in their personal and professional lives. The course garnered widespread acclaim, attracting participants from all walks of life.

Buoyed by her successes, Sarah expanded her business empire. She launched a publishing company dedicated to giving voice to unheard stories, championing authors whose narratives challenged conventional norms and opened doors to new perspectives. She also established a foundation that provided grants and resources to aspiring storytellers from marginalized communities, empowering them to share their unique tales with the world.

Sarah's business empire continued to flourish, driven by her unwavering commitment to the power of storytelling. She knew that everyone had a story to tell and that by sharing these narratives, they could inspire, educate, and bring about positive change.

Her empire became a force for good, a beacon of hope for those who had felt silenced or marginalized. Through her various ventures, Sarah created a ripple effect, empowering others to embrace their own stories and use them as catalysts for personal growth and societal transformation.

As Sarah stood on the rooftop of her company headquarters, overlooking the city that had witnessed her journey, she felt an overwhelming sense of gratitude. Her business empire had not only brought her financial success but had also allowed her to touch countless lives, fostering empathy and understanding in a world that often seemed divided.

Sarah's story serves as a testament to the power of authenticity, resilience, and the human connection. Through her own life experiences, she not only built an empire but also created a movement, reminding us all of the profound impact that our stories can have on the world.

With her business empire firmly established, Sarah embarked on new ventures to expand her reach and influence. Recognizing the growing power of digital media, she launched a podcast where she interviewed individuals from all walks of life, delving into their personal stories and sharing their unique perspectives. The podcast became an instant hit, garnering millions of listeners who eagerly tuned in to be inspired by the authentic voices and diverse experiences shared.

Sarah's keen eye for innovation led her to explore partnerships and collaborations with other creative minds. She joined forces with filmmakers, artists, and musicians, using their talents to bring stories to life through various mediums. Together, they created impactful documentaries, visual art installations, and soul-stirring musical compositions that touched hearts and provoked conversations on important societal issues.

As her influence grew, Sarah's business empire expanded internationally. She established branches and partnerships in different countries, embracing cultural diversity and amplifying the voices of storytellers from all corners of the globe. Her global presence allowed her to bridge gaps and foster understanding between people from different backgrounds, promoting empathy and unity in an increasingly interconnected world.

Sarah's commitment to social responsibility never wavered. She used her resources and platform to address pressing social and environmental issues. Through her foundation, she funded initiatives focused on education, environmental conservation, and social justice.

She became an advocate for marginalized communities, using her influence to raise awareness and drive meaningful change.

Despite her remarkable success, Sarah remained grounded and true to her mission. She continued to share her own story, vulnerabilities, and triumphs, reminding others that their stories mattered and had the power to shape their lives. She encouraged individuals to embrace their authentic selves, celebrate their unique journeys, and find strength in their struggles.

Sarah's business empire became a testament to the transformative power of storytelling. It not only provided her with financial abundance but also gave her a platform to touch lives, ignite passions, and foster a sense of belonging in a world that often felt fragmented.

As Sarah reflected on her journey, she realized that her success was not solely measured by the empire she had built but by the lives she had impacted along the way. She had created a community of storytellers, united by their shared belief in the power of narratives to heal, inspire, and transform.

In the final pages of this chapter, Sarah acknowledged that her journey was far from over. She recognized that the true legacy of her business empire lay not in its size or financial success but in the lasting impact it had on individuals and society as a whole.

With renewed determination, Sarah set her sights on new horizons, knowing that there were still countless stories waiting to be told, and that through them, she could continue to change the world—one narrative at a time.

Every person on this planet has a story to tell. It is the culmination of our unique experiences, joys, sorrows, triumphs, and failures that shape us into the individuals we are today. Your life's journey, with all its twists and turns, has given you a treasure trove of stories to share with the world. In this chapter, we will explore the power of embracing your unique story and how you can use it to inspire, connect, and make a positive impact on others.

Take a moment to reflect on the significant moments and experiences that have shaped your life. It could be the challenges you've overcome, the relationships you've built, or the adventures you've embarked upon. Consider the lessons you've learned and how they have shaped your perspective. Your story is a tapestry woven with the threads of your experiences, and each thread adds depth and richness to the overall narrative.

Sharing your story requires vulnerability—the willingness to open yourself up, exposing both the triumphs and the vulnerabilities. It's through vulnerability that you create a genuine connection with others. Remember that vulnerability is not a weakness; it is a strength.

By sharing your experiences, you give others the courage to embrace their own stories and find solace in knowing that they are not alone.

Within your story lies a powerful message, a lesson that can resonate with others. Reflect on the themes that emerge from your experiences. Is it resilience, compassion, or the pursuit of dreams? Identify the core message you want to convey and the impact you hope to make. Your unique perspective can offer insights, motivate change, or provide comfort to those who are facing similar challenges.

Consider the different mediums through which you can share your story. Writing a book, starting a blog, creating art, or engaging through public speaking are just a few examples. Explore your strengths and interests to find the medium that aligns best with your message and allows you to express yourself authentically.

Sharing your story is an invitation for others to connect with you on a deeper level. Engage with your audience through social media, community events, or support groups. Create spaces for dialogue and foster connections that transcend the boundaries of geography, culture, and background. By sharing your story, you open the door for others to share theirs, fostering empathy, understanding, and a sense of belonging.

As you share your story, remember to honor the journey you've taken. Celebrate your growth and the person you have become. Embrace the lessons learned, both the successes and the setbacks, for they have all contributed to the beautiful tapestry of your life. By acknowledging your journey, you inspire others to see the value in their own experiences and find meaning in their stories.

You have a story to share with the world—a story that can touch hearts, ignite change, and foster connection. Embrace your unique experiences and perspectives, for they are the seeds of inspiration waiting to be sown. Whether your audience is one person or millions, your story matters. Embrace vulnerability, identify your message, choose your medium, and connect with others. Remember that your story has the power to leave a lasting impact, and by sharing it, you can make a positive difference in the lives of others.

Sharing your story with the world can be intimidating. Doubts may arise, questioning whether your experiences are significant enough or if anyone would care to listen. It's important to recognize that your story is unique to you, and there are individuals out there who can relate to and find value in it. Don't let fear hold you back from sharing your truth. Embrace the courage within you, and remember that your story has the potential to inspire, uplift, and empower others.

When sharing your story, authenticity is key. People are drawn to genuine, heartfelt narratives that resonate with their own lives. Embrace your true self and be unapologetically you. Allow your vulnerabilities to shine through, for it is within these vulnerable moments that others can find strength and connection. Trust that your authenticity will create a deeper impact and forge genuine connections with those who encounter your story.

The experiences you've had in life have likely transformed you in various ways. Highlight the personal growth, resilience, and lessons learned throughout your journey. Share how you have overcome adversity, how you've adapted to change, and how you've discovered your own inner strength. By emphasizing the transformative power of your experiences, you inspire others to believe in their own capacity for growth and change.

Your story is a part of your legacy—a gift that can outlast your time on this Earth. Consider the impact you want to make and the lasting impression you want to leave behind. How do you want to be remembered? By sharing your story, you contribute to the collective human experience, adding a unique thread to the fabric of history. Your legacy is not solely defined by your accomplishments, but also by the way you touch the lives of others through the power of storytelling.

As you share your story, remember to embrace the stories of others. Just as your experiences have shaped you, the stories of others have the power to inspire and broaden your understanding of the world. Listen actively and with empathy, for within each person's narrative lies wisdom and insight. Engage in conversations, engage with diverse perspectives, and celebrate the tapestry of human stories that interconnect and weave together.

Your story is ever-evolving, just as you are. Embrace the idea that your experiences and perspectives will continue to evolve and deepen as you navigate through life. Engage in continuous self-reflection, always seeking to learn, grow, and expand your horizons. Embrace new chapters, new adventures, and new lessons that will add depth and richness to your story. Remember that your story is never truly finished but remains a work in progress, with the potential to inspire and touch lives for generations to come.

Your story is a gift, a testament to your unique journey through life. Embrace it wholeheartedly, for within your experiences lies the power to connect, inspire, and create positive change. Overcome fear and doubt, be authentic, emphasize the transformative power of your experiences, and leave a lasting legacy. Embrace the stories of others, and engage in continual growth and reflection. Your story matters, and by sharing it with the world, you contribute to the collective tapestry of human existence. The world is waiting to hear your voice, so go forth and share your remarkable story with confidence and pride.

Reinventing Yourself

In the realm of artistic expression, many creators have adopted alternate identities to encapsulate their works and craft a distinct persona. From authors to musicians, the use of pen names and stage names has become a creative and strategic choice, offering a veil of mystery or a chance to reinvent oneself. In this chapter, we will explore some notable authors who have employed pen names and musicians who have adopted stage names, shedding light on their true identities.

Authors and Their Pen Names:

Mary Ann Evans - George Eliot:

One of the most iconic examples of an author adopting a pen name is Mary Ann Evans, who wrote under the name George Eliot. Born in 1819, Evans published her works during a time when female authors faced significant prejudice. By adopting a male pen name, she hoped to circumvent the biases prevalent in the literary world. Under the guise of George Eliot, Evans produced renowned novels such as "Middlemarch" and "The Mill on the Floss," securing her place in literary history.

Eric Blair - George Orwell:

Eric Blair, known by his pen name George Orwell, is celebrated for his dystopian novels and incisive political commentaries. Orwell adopted a pseudonym to separate his literary identity from his non-fictional work as a journalist. His most famous works, "Nineteen Eighty-Four" and "Animal Farm," under the name George Orwell, have become synonymous with powerful social and political critique.

Joanne Rowling - J.K. Rowling:

In the realm of contemporary literature, J.K. Rowling stands as a prime example of an author who embraced a pen name to navigate the publishing industry. Joanne Rowling, who penned the immensely popular "Harry Potter" series, chose to publish under the gender-neutral initials "J.K." to appeal to a broader audience, especially young boys. The success of her books and subsequent film adaptations propelled her to global fame, making her real identity an open secret.

Musicians and Their Stage Names:

Stefani Germanotta - Lady Gaga:

The multi-talented musician known for her flamboyant style and boundary-pushing performances, Lady Gaga, was born Stefani Germanotta. Adopting her stage name allowed her to craft an eccentric and captivating image while maintaining a level of artistic separation from her personal life. Under the moniker Lady

Gaga, she has released numerous chart-topping hits like "Bad Romance," "Poker Face," and "Born This Way."

Reginald Dwight - Elton John:

Reginald Dwight, a British singer-songwriter, embraced a stage name that has since become synonymous with musical brilliance and flamboyance. Transforming into Elton John, he embarked on a musical journey that produced timeless classics such as "Rocket Man," "Your Song," and "Candle in the Wind." The adoption of a stage name allowed him to transcend his birth name and create an iconic persona in the world of music.

Alecia Beth Moore - Pink:

Known for her powerful vocals and rebellious attitude, Pink, born Alecia Beth Moore, opted for a stage name that exuded confidence and individuality. By adopting a single-word stage name, she successfully branded herself as a unique force in the pop-rock genre. Pink's hits like "Just Like a Pill," "So What," and "Raise Your Glass" have propelled her to international stardom.

The utilization of pen names and stage names has long been a part of artistic expression, allowing authors and musicians to navigate the complexities of their industries and establish distinct identities. From Mary Ann Evans, who became George Eliot, to Stefani Germanotta, who became Lady Gaga, these individuals strategically selected alternative identities to shape their creative personas and connect with their audiences in a profound way.

The decision to use pen names and stage names serves several purposes for artists. Firstly, it provides a sense of anonymity and detachment from their personal lives, allowing them to explore various artistic avenues without the constraints of societal expectations or preconceived notions. By adopting a different name, artists can experiment, take risks, and delve into new creative territories while maintaining a certain level of privacy.

Secondly, pen names and stage names can be powerful branding tools. They enable artists to craft a distinctive image and persona that resonates with their artistic vision and the themes they wish to explore in their work. These names become part of the artistic package, evoking emotions, capturing attention, and creating a lasting impression on their audience.

Moreover, adopting a pseudonym can be a strategic move to overcome societal biases or barriers prevalent in the creative industries. Female authors like Mary Ann Evans, who chose George Eliot as her pen name, sought to circumvent the gender-based prejudices that hindered their recognition and acceptance in the literary world. By taking on a male pseudonym, they could ensure their works were judged on their merits rather than their gender.

Similarly, musicians often adopt stage names to enhance their marketability and create a distinct identity within the highly competitive music industry. Stage names allow artists to stand out from the crowd, capturing the attention of listeners and fostering a connection with their fans. It enables them to embody a larger-than-life persona, often associated with their unique style, sound, or genre.

It is worth noting that the decision to reveal the true identities behind these pen names and stage names is a personal choice for the artists involved. Some authors and musicians eventually choose to disclose their real names, allowing their audience to gain a deeper understanding of the person behind the art. However, for many artists, maintaining the separation between their public personas and personal lives remains a crucial aspect of their artistic expression and creative journey.

The use of pen names and stage names has been a recurring phenomenon among authors and musicians throughout history. Whether employed for creative liberation, branding purposes, or to overcome societal barriers, these alternative identities serve as powerful tools for artists to shape their artistic narratives and forge meaningful connections with their audiences.

In the journey of life, we often encounter moments when we feel the need to break free from the confines of our current selves and embark on a path of reinvention. The power of reinventing oneself lies in the transformative process of shedding old layers, exploring new possibilities, and aligning our actions with our goals and aspirations. In this chapter, we delve into the significance of reinvention and how it can propel us towards personal growth and the fulfillment of our deepest desires.

Reinvention requires embracing change wholeheartedly. It demands a willingness to let go of the familiar and venture into uncharted territories. By recognizing that change is an inherent part of life, we can overcome the fear and resistance that often accompany the process. Embracing change allows us to break free from self-imposed limitations and opens doors to opportunities we might not have otherwise considered.

Reinvention requires challenging and releasing the limiting beliefs that have held us back. These beliefs often stem from societal expectations, past failures, or self-doubt. By examining and reframing our belief systems, we can dismantle the barriers that hinder our progress. Reinvention provides an opportunity to redefine ourselves and cultivate empowering beliefs that align with our goals and dreams.

Reinvention invites us to embark on a journey of self-discovery. It is a process of introspection, where we delve into our passions, values, and deepest desires. By reconnecting with our authentic selves, we gain clarity about what truly matters to us and what we aspire to achieve. Self-discovery allows us to identify the areas of our lives that need transformation and helps us set meaningful goals that resonate with our core essence.

Reinvention necessitates flexibility and adaptability. As we chart a new course, we must be open to unexpected twists and turns, adjusting our plans and strategies as needed. This ability to adapt ensures that we remain resilient in the face of challenges and setbacks. Flexibility allows us to explore different paths, embrace opportunities, and seize the moment when it presents itself.

Reinvention is not a one-time event; it is an ongoing process. As we evolve, our goals and aspirations may change, requiring us to continually adapt and reinvent ourselves. Each reinvention builds upon the lessons and experiences of the past, leading to personal growth and the refinement of our true selves. It is a dynamic journey of self-improvement and self-realization.

Reinvention often encounters resistance, both from within ourselves and from external sources. Our inner critic may question our abilities and worthiness of change, while others may resist our transformation, fearing the disruption it may cause. Overcoming resistance requires perseverance, resilience, and a strong belief in ourselves and our vision. It is essential to surround ourselves with supportive individuals who understand and encourage our journey of reinvention.

The power of reinvention lies in its ability to open up a world of possibilities. It allows us to explore new passions, careers, relationships, and experiences. By reinventing ourselves, we expand our horizons, tap into our untapped potential, and create a life that aligns with our authentic selves. Embracing possibilities fuels our sense of purpose and ignites the fire within us to pursue our goals with passion and determination.

Reinventing oneself is a transformative process that empowers individuals to break free from limitations, embrace change, and align their actions with their goals and aspirations. It is a journey of self-discovery, flexibility, and growth, requiring courage, resilience, and a willingness to let go of the familiar. The power of reinvention lies in its ability to propel us towards personal growth, fulfillment, and the realization of our true potential.

Reinvention offers us the opportunity to shed old identities and narratives that no longer serve us. It allows us to step out of our comfort zones and explore new facets of ourselves. Through reinvention, we can tap into hidden talents, develop new skills, and discover passions we never knew existed. By embracing change and self-discovery, we can uncover the depths of our abilities and unlock doors to previously unimagined possibilities.

Furthermore, reinvention provides a fresh perspective on life and its challenges. It enables us to view obstacles as opportunities for growth and learning. Rather than succumbing to fear or giving in to self-doubt, we can approach challenges with resilience and an open mind. Reinvention allows us to adapt to new circumstances, find innovative solutions, and cultivate a sense of adaptability that serves us well in an ever-changing world.

Reinvention also allows us to align our lives with our true values and aspirations. It offers an opportunity to evaluate our priorities and make conscious choices that support our goals. By reevaluating our relationships, career paths, and lifestyle choices, we can ensure that they are in harmony with our authentic selves. Reinvention empowers us to design a life that reflects our deepest desires and values, leading to a greater sense of fulfillment and purpose.

Moreover, the process of reinvention can inspire and influence others. When we boldly embrace change and pursue our dreams, we become living examples of the transformative power of reinvention. By sharing our journey and the lessons we have learned, we can inspire others to embark on their own paths of self-discovery and reinvention. Our stories become a testament to the human capacity for growth and resilience, igniting a ripple effect of positive change in our communities and beyond.

It is important to remember that reinvention is a personal journey, and each individual's path will be unique. There is no one-size-fits-all approach to reinvention, as it is deeply intertwined with our individual values, aspirations, and circumstances. It requires self-reflection, introspection, and a willingness to take risks. It may involve seeking guidance from mentors, acquiring new knowledge and skills, or making difficult choices. However, the rewards of reinvention—personal growth, fulfillment, and living a life aligned with our true selves—are worth the effort and challenges along the way.

The power of reinvention lies in its ability to transform our lives and help us achieve our goals. By embracing change, letting go of limiting beliefs, and embracing new possibilities, we can tap into our true potential and design a life that aligns with our deepest aspirations. Through reinvention, we can break free from the constraints of our past and create a future that reflects our authentic selves, paving the way for personal growth, fulfillment, and a life of purpose.

"What Do You Love?"

Life is a journey filled with endless possibilities and opportunities. It is a quest to find what truly brings us joy, fulfillment, and a sense of purpose. While the path to self-discovery may not always be straightforward, it is a journey worth embarking upon. In this chapter, we will explore ways to help you uncover what you love most in life, allowing you to live a more passionate and meaningful existence.

Curiosity is the compass that leads us to new experiences and insights. Open your mind to the world around you and be willing to explore different interests, hobbies, and subjects. Engage in activities that pique your curiosity, whether it's reading books, attending workshops, or joining clubs. Allow yourself the freedom to discover what excites you, for it is often in the pursuit of knowledge and new experiences that we stumble upon our true passions.

Take a moment to reflect on your past experiences and identify moments when you felt genuinely happy and fulfilled. What were you doing during those moments? Was it helping others, creating something, solving a problem, or expressing yourself? Delve deep into these memories and consider the underlying factors that made those experiences special. Reflecting on the past can provide valuable insights into what truly resonates with your heart and soul.

When something captures your attention and ignites your curiosity, follow it. Don't be afraid to explore uncharted territories or take risks. Follow the breadcrumbs of your interests, for they often lead to unexpected discoveries. Allow yourself the freedom to dive deep into subjects and activities that captivate your imagination. Remember, it's not just about the destination but also the journey of self-discovery along the way.

Carve out moments of solitude and engage in self-reflection. Create a space where you can disconnect from the noise and demands of the outside world. Ask yourself thought-provoking questions like, "What are my values and beliefs? What brings me the greatest joy? What activities make me lose track of time?" By delving into these introspective inquiries, you will gain valuable insights into what truly matters to you.

Finding what you love most in life is not always a linear path. There may be detours, setbacks, and failures along the way. Embrace these moments as opportunities for growth and learning. Understand that failure is not an endpoint but a stepping stone towards success. Be adaptable and willing to pivot when necessary. By viewing challenges as learning experiences, you will develop resilience and discover valuable lessons that will guide you closer to your passions.

Surround yourself with people who inspire and uplift you. Seek out mentors, friends, or communities that align with your interests and aspirations. Engaging with like-minded individuals can provide encouragement, guidance, and support on your journey. Share your aspirations and dreams with others, for they may offer unique perspectives and opportunities that can lead you closer to what you love most in life.

Discovering what you love most in life is a continuous journey of self-exploration, curiosity, and personal growth. Embrace the process, trust your instincts, and be open to the unexpected. Remember that life's true treasures are often found in the pursuit of our passions. Embrace the beauty of self-discovery and allow your authentic self to shine through as you uncover what brings you the most joy, fulfillment, and purpose in life.

To discover what you love most in life, embrace novelty and step out of your comfort zone. Try new activities, visit new places, and meet new people. Novel experiences can provide fresh perspectives and awaken hidden passions within you. Say yes to opportunities that come your way, even if they seem unfamiliar or challenging. It is through these new encounters that you may stumble upon something extraordinary that resonates deeply with your being.

Pay attention to the activities and experiences that energize you versus those that drain you. Notice how you feel before, during, and after engaging in different pursuits. Activities that align with your passions often leave you feeling invigorated, enthusiastic, and fulfilled. Conversely, activities that don't resonate with your true desires may leave you feeling depleted and unfulfilled. Tune in to your energy levels as an indicator of what brings you genuine joy and enthusiasm.

Considering the amount of time we spend working, it's essential to explore career paths that align with our passions. If you're unsure about your true calling, don't be afraid to explore different professions. Volunteer, intern, or take on part-time roles in fields that interest you. Seek mentorship from professionals who have found fulfillment in their careers. By actively exploring various career paths, you'll gain valuable insights into what truly sparks your enthusiasm and ignites your professional drive.

The journey of self-discovery can be filled with moments of self-doubt, uncertainty, and frustration. It's important to cultivate self-compassion throughout this process. Be kind and patient with yourself. Understand that discovering your true passions takes time and experimentation. Embrace the process of exploration without judgment or comparison to others. Celebrate small victories and learn from setbacks. By treating yourself with kindness and compassion, you create a nurturing environment for self-discovery and growth.

In the midst of the noise and expectations of the world, it's crucial to listen to your intuition—the quiet voice within you that knows your deepest desires. Pay attention to the subtle nudges and gut feelings that arise when you encounter something meaningful. Your intuition serves as a compass, guiding you towards what aligns with your authentic self. Trust your inner guidance and allow it to lead you towards what you love most in life.

Never stop learning and expanding your horizons. Engage in lifelong learning by seeking knowledge and skills related to your interests. Take courses, attend workshops, read books, and engage in discussions with experts in fields that captivate your curiosity. The more you learn, the more you refine your understanding of what truly resonates with you. Through continuous learning, you deepen your expertise and nourish your passions.

Discovering what you love most in life is a dynamic and ongoing process. It requires self-exploration, courage, and an open mind. Embrace curiosity, reflect on past experiences, follow your intuition, and be open to new possibilities. Remember that the discovery of your passions is not an endpoint but a lifelong journey of self-discovery and growth. As you embark on this quest, stay true to yourself, cultivate self-compassion, and trust that by pursuing what brings you joy and fulfillment, you will create a life that is truly meaningful and rewarding.

Passions are the sparks that ignite our souls and propel us forward on the journey of life. They are the driving forces behind our creativity, purpose, and fulfillment. In this chapter, we will explore the idea that your passions are your greatest assets in life. By recognizing and embracing your passions, you unlock a world of possibilities and tap into the immense power within you.

Passion is a wellspring of motivation. When you are genuinely passionate about something, you naturally feel inspired and driven to take action. Your passions give you a sense of purpose and a direction in life. They provide the fuel that propels you forward, even in the face of challenges. By harnessing the power of your passions, you tap into an unlimited reserve of motivation that can help you overcome obstacles and achieve remarkable feats.

Passion and resilience go hand in hand. When you are passionate about something, setbacks and failures become mere stepping stones on the path to success. Your deep-rooted love for your passions gives you the strength and determination to persevere through difficult times. It fuels your resilience and enables you to bounce back from setbacks with renewed vigor. Your passions become a source of inner strength, empowering you to overcome obstacles and forge ahead on your chosen path.

Passion is the driving force behind innovation and creativity. When you are truly passionate about something, you approach it with a fresh perspective and a willingness to explore uncharted territories. Your passions ignite your curiosity, leading you to discover new ideas, methods, and solutions. By leveraging your passions, you become a catalyst for innovation in your chosen field, making unique contributions and leaving a lasting impact.

When you engage in activities that align with your passions, you enter a state of flow—a state of optimal performance and deep immersion. Time seems to fade away, and you become fully absorbed in what you are doing. This heightened state of focus and concentration allows you to perform at your best, tapping into your natural talents and abilities. Your passions enhance your performance by enabling you to operate in a state of heightened productivity, creativity, and excellence.

True fulfillment in life comes from living in alignment with your passions. When you pursue what you love, you experience a deep sense of satisfaction and joy. Your passions provide a sense of purpose and meaning, connecting you with your authentic self and the world around you. By embracing your passions, you create a life that is rich with fulfillment and contentment.

Your passions become the guiding light that leads you to a life well-lived.

Your passions have the power to inspire and influence those around you. When you wholeheartedly pursue what you love, you radiate enthusiasm and authenticity. Your passion becomes infectious, motivating others to explore their own passions and live with purpose. By sharing your passions and the knowledge you gain from pursuing them, you become a source of inspiration and encouragement to others, creating a ripple effect of positive change in the world.

Your passions are not mere hobbies or fleeting interests; they are your greatest assets in life. They fuel your motivation, breed resilience, drive innovation, enhance performance, ignite fulfillment, and inspire others. Embrace your passions unapologetically and make them a central part of your life. They are the keys that unlock the door to a life of purpose, joy, and meaningful impact. Your passions are uniquely yours, and by nurturing and honoring them, you unlock your true potential and create a legacy that is authentically yours.

Finding the Formula

In the journey of entrepreneurship, finding your own unique formula for success is crucial. It's not about blindly following someone else's path or trying to imitate their strategies. It's about discovering what truly works for you, your business, and your target audience. In this chapter, we will delve into the process of finding your own unique formula for success in your business.

Success starts with a clear vision of what you want to achieve. Take some time to define your long-term goals, both personally and professionally. Consider what impact you want to make, what values you want to uphold, and the legacy you want to leave behind. This vision will guide you in creating a unique formula for success that aligns with your aspirations.

Reflect on your own strengths and passions. What are you exceptionally good at? What do you enjoy doing the most? By identifying these areas, you can leverage them in your business and capitalize on what sets you apart from others. Your strengths and passions will be the foundation of your unique formula for success.

To create a successful business, you must have a deep understanding of your target audience. Conduct thorough market research to identify their needs, desires, pain points, and preferences. What problems can you solve for them? How can you provide value? By understanding your target audience, you can tailor your unique formula to cater specifically to their needs.

While it's important not to copy your competitors, analyzing their strategies can provide valuable insights. Identify successful businesses within your industry and examine what they are doing differently. What sets them apart? Look for gaps or untapped opportunities in the market that you can explore and develop in your own unique way.

To find your unique formula for success, you must be open to creativity and innovation. Explore unconventional approaches, challenge the status quo, and think outside the box. Consider how you can differentiate your products, services, or processes in a way that captures the attention of your target audience. Innovate to solve problems in a manner that is distinct and memorable.

Once you have formulated a unique approach, it's essential to test and iterate. Implement your strategies on a small scale, gather feedback, and measure the results. Be open to adjustments and improvements along the way. Success is often a result of continuous learning and adaptation.

Refine your formula based on what works and discard what doesn't.

Authenticity is a key ingredient in any successful business formula. Be true to yourself, your values, and your vision. Don't try to imitate others or pretend to be someone you're not. People appreciate and resonate with authenticity, and it will help you build trust and long-lasting relationships with your customers.

The journey towards success is a lifelong learning process. Stay curious, seek knowledge, and invest in your personal and professional growth. Attend seminars, workshops, and conferences related to your industry. Surround yourself with mentors and like-minded individuals who can provide guidance and support. Continuously refining and expanding your knowledge will contribute to the evolution of your unique formula for success.

Finding your own unique formula for success in your business requires self-reflection, market understanding, creativity, and adaptability. By defining your vision, leveraging your strengths, understanding your audience, and embracing innovation, you can create a formula that sets you apart from others. Remember, success is not an endpoint but an ongoing journey of growth and development.

A growth mindset is crucial for uncovering your unique formula for success. Embrace challenges as opportunities for growth rather than obstacles. See failures as learning experiences that propel you forward. Believe in your ability to learn, adapt, and improve. A growth mindset will enable you to approach your business with resilience, perseverance, and a willingness to explore new possibilities.

Success in business is often built on strong relationships. Cultivate a network of connections that can support and inspire you. Collaborate with like-minded individuals and complementary businesses. Surround yourself with mentors, advisors, and peers who can provide valuable insights and guidance. Remember that success is rarely achieved alone, and nurturing relationships will open doors to new opportunities.

Your customers are the lifeblood of your business, so prioritize their experience. Understand their journey, anticipate their needs, and exceed their expectations. Provide exceptional customer service and build meaningful connections. By putting your customers at the center of your unique formula, you create a positive reputation and loyal following that sets you apart from your competitors.

The business landscape is constantly evolving, driven by technological advancements and shifting consumer preferences. Stay attuned to emerging trends in your industry and adapt accordingly. Embrace innovation and embrace new technologies that can enhance your products, services, or processes. By staying ahead of the curve, you can position your business as a leader and maintain a competitive edge.

Success is measurable, so establish key metrics that align with your business goals. Regularly monitor and analyze these metrics to track your progress and make data-driven decisions. Identify areas of improvement, celebrate milestones, and adjust your strategies as needed. By staying informed about your business's performance, you can make informed decisions that contribute to your unique formula for success.

In today's fast-paced business environment, agility and flexibility are vital. Embrace a mindset of adaptability and be open to change. Remain nimble and willing to pivot your strategies if necessary. By being responsive to market demands and consumer feedback, you can adjust your unique formula to stay relevant and meet evolving needs.

Amidst the pursuit of success, it's essential to celebrate your wins, both big and small. Acknowledge and appreciate your accomplishments along the way. This fosters a positive mindset and fuels your motivation to continue striving for greater heights. Recognize the progress you've made and use it as fuel to propel yourself forward.

Finding your unique formula for success in your business is a dynamic and ongoing process. It requires self-reflection, market understanding, creativity, adaptability, and a growth mindset. By cultivating strong relationships, prioritizing customer experience, monitoring key metrics, and embracing agility, you can continuously refine and enhance your formula. Remember, your unique formula for success is a reflection of your values, strengths, and aspirations, and it will continue to evolve as you grow both personally and professionally. Embrace the journey, learn from every experience, and let your unique formula guide you to extraordinary achievements.

Reaching Your Audience

It's a great, big world out there. It's time for you to take center stage. In the world of online business, reaching your target audience is essential for success. Whether you're selling products, offering services, or sharing valuable content, understanding and connecting with your target audience is crucial. In this chapter, we will explore effective strategies and techniques to help you reach and engage your target audience effectively.

Before you can reach your target audience, you need to clearly define who they are. Start by creating buyer personas that represent your ideal customers. Consider demographics such as age, gender, location, interests, and online behaviors.

This will help you understand their needs, preferences, and pain points, allowing you to tailor your marketing efforts accordingly.

Market research is essential for gaining insights into your target audience. Use various methods like surveys, interviews, and social media analytics to gather information. Analyze competitor strategies, industry trends, and consumer behavior to identify gaps and opportunities within your niche. This research will provide a solid foundation for your marketing strategy.

To attract your target audience, you must establish a strong brand identity that resonates with them. Create a unique brand voice, visual elements, and messaging that align with your audience's values and aspirations. Consistency across your website, social media platforms, and marketing materials will help you build recognition and trust among your target audience.

Search engine optimization (SEO) plays a vital role in reaching your target audience. Conduct keyword research to identify the terms and phrases your audience uses when searching for products or services like yours. Incorporate these keywords strategically into your website's content, meta tags, headings, and URLs. Focus on creating high-quality, relevant content that provides value to your audience.

Social media platforms provide an excellent opportunity to connect with your target audience. Identify the platforms where your audience is most active and create a strong presence there. Share engaging content, interact with your audience, and join relevant communities or groups. Leverage paid advertising options on platforms like Facebook, Instagram, or LinkedIn to reach a wider audience that matches your target demographics.

Content marketing allows you to showcase your expertise, attract your target audience, and build trust. Create valuable, informative, and entertaining content such as blog posts, videos, podcasts, or infographics that cater to your audience's interests and needs. Optimize your content for SEO and share it across your website, social media platforms, and relevant online communities.

Building an email list is a powerful way to reach your target audience directly. Offer valuable incentives like exclusive content, discounts, or free resources to encourage visitors to subscribe. Segment your email list based on demographics, interests, or purchase history to deliver personalized content and offers. Regularly send engaging newsletters, product updates, or special promotions to keep your audience engaged.

Influencer marketing has become a popular strategy to reach target audiences. Identify influencers within your niche who have a strong following and credibility with your target audience. Collaborate with them through sponsored posts, guest blogging, or joint promotions. Their endorsement and reach can significantly boost your visibility and credibility among your target audience.

Additionally, always strive for authenticity and transparency in your marketing efforts. Today's consumers value brands that are genuine and relatable. Build trust by being honest, providing valuable content, and delivering on your promises. This will foster a loyal following and encourage your audience to become advocates for your business.

Don't underestimate the power of word-of-mouth marketing. Encourage your satisfied customers to share their experiences with others and provide testimonials or reviews. Positive word-of-mouth can be a powerful driver of growth, as people are more likely to trust recommendations from friends or family.

Reaching your target audience in your online business is a multifaceted endeavor that requires a deep understanding of your audience, a strong brand identity, and effective marketing strategies. By defining your target audience, conducting market research, optimizing your website, utilizing social media, implementing content marketing and email marketing, collaborating with influencers, and consistently analyzing and refining your approach, you will be well on your way to reaching and engaging your desired audience. Stay adaptable, authentic, and attentive to your audience's needs, and you will establish a strong connection that drives the success of your online business.

Social media has become an integral part of our daily lives, presenting a vast opportunity for businesses to increase their visibility and reach a broader audience. In this chapter, we will explore effective strategies to boost your online visibility using social media platforms. We'll provide examples of successful brands that have leveraged social media to enhance their visibility and engage with their target audience.

Not all social media platforms are created equal, and it's essential to identify the platforms where your target audience is most active. For example:

With over 2.8 billion monthly active users, Facebook is suitable for businesses targeting a wide range of demographics. Example: Coca-Cola utilizes Facebook to engage with its audience by sharing captivating visual content, running contests, and leveraging user-generated content.

Known for its visually appealing content, Instagram is popular among younger demographics and businesses in visually-oriented industries. Example: Nike leverages Instagram to showcase its products, collaborate with influencers, and engage with its passionate community through inspiring and aspirational content.

As a professional networking platform, LinkedIn is ideal for B2B businesses and those targeting professionals. Example: Microsoft utilizes LinkedIn to share thought leadership articles, job opportunities, and industry updates, positioning itself as a leader in the tech industry.

With its fast-paced, real-time nature, Twitter is suitable for businesses that want to share news, engage in conversations, and provide customer support. Example: Wendy's, a fast-food chain, gained visibility through witty and humorous interactions with its audience, creating a distinct brand voice and driving engagement.

To increase visibility on social media, you need to create compelling content that captures the attention of your audience. Images, videos, and infographics tend to perform well on social media. Use high-quality visuals that align with your brand and resonate with your audience. Example: Red Bull produces visually stunning and adrenaline-inducing videos that highlight extreme sports and adventure.

Social media is not just about broadcasting content; it's also a platform for conversation and engagement. Here are some ways to foster interaction:

Actively engage with your audience by responding to comments, messages, and mentions. This shows that you value their input and helps build relationships. Example: Zappos, an online shoe and clothing retailer, is known for its excellent customer service on social media, promptly addressing customer inquiries and providing support.

Use features like Facebook Live, Instagram Live, or Twitter Spaces to host live events, Q&A sessions, or webinars. This allows real-time interaction with your audience and builds trust and credibility. Example: Sephora regularly hosts live beauty tutorials and Q&A sessions with makeup artists and beauty influencers to educate and engage their audience.

Participate in Relevant Conversations. Join industry-related conversations, use hashtags, and participate in trending topics to increase your visibility. This positions you as an active and knowledgeable participant in your industry. Example: Oreo, the popular cookie brand, often joins trending conversations by creating timely and clever social media posts, gaining attention and engagement from their audience.

While organic reach on social media is valuable, leveraging paid advertising can significantly enhance your visibility. Consider the following advertising options:

Use Facebook's robust targeting options to reach your specific audience based on demographics, interests, and behaviors. Example: Airbnb uses Facebook ads to target users interested in travel and vacation rentals, showcasing their unique accommodations and experiences.

Leverage Instagram's visually-driven platform to promote your products or services. Use features like carousel ads or story ads to engage your audience. Example: Fashion brand H&M runs sponsored ads on Instagram, showcasing their latest collections and driving traffic to their online store.

First Impressions

First impressions are lasting impressions. When you meet the world, be prepared to put your best foot forward. In the grand tapestry of human interactions, few things carry as much weight as the first impression. Whether we realize it or not, we are constantly forming judgments about others within seconds of meeting them. These initial perceptions set the tone for our relationships, shape our interactions, and can leave a lasting impact on both personal and professional endeavors. Understanding the significance of making a good first impression is the key to unlocking a world of opportunities and forging meaningful connections. So, let us delve into the power of first impressions and learn how to harness this influence to our advantage.

Human beings are hardwired to form snap judgments, a remnant of our evolutionary instincts. When encountering someone new, our brains quickly categorize and evaluate based on visual cues, body language, and demeanor. Research suggests that we form initial impressions within a mere seven seconds of meeting someone. In those fleeting moments, we determine factors such as trustworthiness, competence, likability, and attractiveness. Such swift judgments serve as a filter for our interactions, guiding our subsequent behavior and shaping our perception of the person we have just met.

First impressions have a domino effect on how we perceive others. Psychologists refer to this phenomenon as the "Halo Effect." When we perceive someone positively upon first meeting them, we tend to attribute other positive qualities to them as well. For instance, if we find someone to be friendly and approachable, we are more likely to assume they are also intelligent and capable. This cognitive bias influences our thoughts, opinions, and subsequent interactions, creating a self-fulfilling prophecy that reinforces our initial impression.

While it is true that first impressions are formed rapidly, their impact can endure for an extended period. Research indicates that it takes far more subsequent positive experiences to overturn a negative first impression. This is due to our natural inclination to seek consistency and confirmation bias. Once we have formed an initial perception, we tend to interpret subsequent actions and behaviors in a way that aligns with our original judgment. Therefore, making a good first impression becomes even more crucial as it sets the foundation for building trust, credibility, and rapport.

The significance of first impressions extends beyond personal relationships and spills over into the professional realm. Job interviews, client meetings, and networking events are prime examples of situations where making a positive initial impact can greatly influence the outcome. Employers and colleagues often use first impressions to evaluate a candidate's suitability for a role, their level of professionalism, and their overall demeanor. Demonstrating confidence, competence, and warmth from the get-go can open doors to career opportunities, collaborations, and promotions.

Crafting a good first impression does not imply putting on a facade or being disingenuous. Authenticity is a key component of making a lasting impact. However, it is essential to be aware of the image we project and the signals we send out. Confidence, genuine interest, positive body language, and appropriate attire all contribute to a favorable impression. Preparation is equally crucial, as it allows us to enter a situation with self-assurance, knowledge, and a clear understanding of the context. By paying attention to these aspects, we can ensure that our authentic selves shine through in the best possible light.

The power of first impressions extends beyond our immediate encounters. The impressions we make on others can influence their opinions, attitudes, and behavior toward us. This ripple effect can expand our network, attract new opportunities, and lead to unforeseen connections. By consistently making positive first impressions, we create a virtuous cycle where our reputation precedes us, opening doors and paving the way for success.

In essence, the importance of making a good first impression lies in the countless doors it can open and the endless possibilities it can create. Whether we aim to establish meaningful personal relationships or advance professionally, understanding and harnessing the power of first impressions is a skill worth mastering. Here are a few additional insights to help you navigate this realm:

Being mindful of our own behavior and empathetic towards others are essential elements of making a positive first impression. By paying attention to our words, tone, and body language, we can ensure that we convey respect, openness, and sincerity. Similarly, actively listening to others, showing genuine interest, and responding thoughtfully help us forge connections based on mutual understanding and respect.

First impressions are not fixed or immutable. They can be improved upon with self-reflection, learning, and growth. Taking the time to evaluate our past interactions and seeking feedback from trusted sources can provide valuable insights into areas for improvement. By continuously refining our communication skills, self-awareness, and emotional intelligence, we can enhance our ability to make positive first impressions.

While making a good first impression is important, it should not be an end in itself. The true value lies in building genuine and meaningful connections with others. Fostering authentic relationships requires consistent effort, mutual respect, and shared experiences. It is through these connections that we can find support, collaboration, and personal fulfillment.

The power of first impressions cannot be underestimated. They shape our relationships, influence opportunities, and define how others perceive us. By understanding the significance of these initial encounters and honing our skills in making positive impressions, we can unlock a world of possibilities and forge lasting connections. Remember, every interaction is an opportunity to make a difference, so approach each one with intention, authenticity, and the willingness to leave a positive and indelible mark.

The pursuit of making good first impressions can serve as a catalyst for personal growth and development. It encourages us to refine our communication skills, cultivate self-awareness, and become more conscious of the impact we have on others. As we strive to make positive impressions, we also learn valuable lessons about empathy, adaptability, and the importance of genuine connections.

Making a good first impression is an art that can transform our personal and professional lives. It opens doors, builds trust, and influences the perceptions of others. By recognizing the significance of these initial encounters, investing in self-improvement, and approaching each interaction with authenticity and intention, we can harness the power of first impressions to create meaningful connections and unlock a world of opportunities.

Invest in Your Dream

Congratulations on starting your online business. In today's digital age, having a strong online presence is crucial for success. As you embark on this entrepreneurial journey, it's important to recognize the value of investing in your online business. In this chapter, we will explore three key areas where investing can make a significant impact: cover design, logo design, and outsourcing. By understanding the importance of these elements and making informed decisions, you will set your online business on the path to prosperity.

First impressions matter, especially in the online world where attention spans are limited. One of the first things potential customers notice about your business is your cover design. Whether it's for an e-book, a product, or a website, investing in high-quality cover design can significantly impact your success.

A visually appealing and professional cover design captures attention and entices people to explore further. It conveys credibility, expertise, and a sense of quality. Remember, customers are more likely to trust and engage with a business that invests in its presentation.

A well-designed cover is an opportunity to showcase your brand identity and establish a strong visual presence. It sets you apart from the competition and creates a consistent experience for your customers. Invest in a cover design that reflects your brand's values, target audience, and unique selling points.

A logo is a visual representation of your business and serves as a powerful symbol of recognition and trust. Investing in professional logo design can have a profound impact on your online business.

A carefully crafted logo helps customers identify your business quickly. It becomes a visual anchor that triggers associations with your products or services. Consistently using your logo across various platforms strengthens brand recognition, making it easier for customers to remember and choose your business over others.

A professional logo design adds credibility and professionalism to your online presence. It instills trust in potential customers and conveys that you are serious about your business. By investing in a high-quality logo, you signal your commitment to excellence, which can significantly impact customer trust and loyalty.

As an entrepreneur, it's essential to focus on your core strengths and delegate tasks that others can handle more efficiently. Outsourcing certain aspects of your online business allows you to save time, tap into specialized expertise, and accelerate growth.

Investing in outsourcing frees up your time and energy to focus on strategic activities that directly impact your business's growth. By delegating tasks such as web design, content creation, or customer support to skilled professionals, you can streamline operations and ensure higher-quality outcomes.

Outsourcing provides an opportunity to leverage the expertise of professionals in various fields. Whether it's graphic design, website development, or marketing, working with specialists who have a deep understanding of their craft can yield exceptional results. Consider outsourcing to take advantage of their knowledge and experience.

Investing in your online business is a key driver of success in today's competitive landscape. By recognizing the importance of cover design, logo design, and outsourcing, you position yourself for growth, differentiation, and increased customer trust. Remember, investing in your business is an ongoing process, and as you continue to evolve, be open to exploring new avenues for investment that align with your goals. Together, these investments will lay the foundation for a thriving online business.

Your website serves as the virtual storefront for your online business, making it a critical component of your success. Investing in professional website design can enhance user experience, drive conversions, and establish credibility.

Investing in content marketing, such as blog posts, videos, and infographics, establishes you as an authoritative source in your industry. By providing valuable and relevant content to your target audience, you can build trust, drive organic traffic to your website, and cultivate a loyal customer base. Remember, high-quality content that educates, entertains, or solves problems is a long-term investment that pays off in brand recognition and customer loyalty.

Investing in your online business is a strategic decision that can yield significant returns. By focusing on cover design, logo design, outsourcing, website design, and marketing, you create a solid foundation for success. Remember, each investment should align with your business goals and target audience. Continuously evaluate and adapt your strategies as your business evolves to stay ahead of the competition. Embrace the power of investing, and watch your online business flourish in the digital landscape.

In the world of business, the old adage "you have to spend money to make money" holds true. While it may seem counterintuitive to part with your hard-earned cash, strategic investments can be the catalyst for growth and success. In this chapter, we will explore the concept of investing in your business and discuss how spending money wisely can lead to long-term profitability.

Investing in the right technology and equipment can significantly improve productivity and efficiency. Whether it's upgrading your computer systems, purchasing specialized software, or acquiring machinery, these investments can streamline operations, reduce costs, and position your business for scalability.

For brick-and-mortar businesses, physical infrastructure investments are crucial. Renovating or expanding your workspace, improving the layout, or enhancing the aesthetics can create a more inviting environment for customers, leading to increased foot traffic and higher sales.

In today's digital landscape, investing in digital marketing strategies is essential for reaching your target audience. Allocating resources to search engine optimization (SEO), pay-per-click (PPC) advertising, social media marketing, and content creation can help generate leads, drive website traffic, and boost conversions.

While digital marketing dominates, traditional advertising methods such as print ads, radio spots, and television commercials still hold value in certain industries. Investing in these channels can help you tap into specific demographics or reach audiences that may not be as active online.

Investing in employee development programs and training initiatives can have a substantial impact on your business. By equipping your workforce with the skills and knowledge needed to excel in their roles, you foster a culture of continuous improvement and increase employee loyalty and productivity.

Recruiting and hiring top talent often requires financial investment. While it may be tempting to cut corners in this area, investing in qualified and experienced employees can pay off in the long run. They bring expertise, innovative ideas, and a dedication to your business's success, elevating the overall performance of your team.

Investing in market research allows you to gain valuable insights into your target audience, industry trends, and customer preferences. This knowledge helps you make informed decisions, identify untapped opportunities, and stay ahead of the competition.

Continuously investing in research and development (R&D) ensures that your products or services remain relevant and competitive. By seeking ways to improve existing offerings or developing new solutions, you can attract new customers, retain existing ones, and open doors to new revenue streams.

While it may be tempting to minimize expenses, strategic investments are essential for long-term business growth and success. By allocating resources to infrastructure, marketing, employee development, and research and development, you position your business for increased profitability, scalability, and competitive advantage. Remember, smart investments require careful consideration, aligning with your business goals and target audience. Embrace the art of investing, and watch as your business thrives and flourishes in the ever-evolving marketplace.

The Marketplace

Congratulations on your decision to venture into the world of online marketplaces! Creating and selling products can be a lucrative way to build wealth and achieve financial independence. In this chapter, we'll explore the essential steps you need to follow to create profitable products for online marketplaces. By understanding your target audience, conducting market research, and leveraging your unique skills and creativity, you'll be well on your way to success.

Before diving into product creation, it's crucial to identify your target audience. Understanding your potential customers' needs, preferences, and pain points will guide your product development process. Consider demographic factors, such as age, gender, location, and interests. Conduct surveys, engage in online communities, and perform market research to gain insights into their desires and challenges.

Thorough market research is the foundation for successful product creation. Analyze existing products in your chosen niche and identify gaps or areas for improvement. Look for trends, popular keywords, and customer reviews to gather valuable information. Utilize online tools like Google Trends, keyword planners, and social listening platforms to gain insights into the market demand.

Armed with market research, it's time to brainstorm product ideas that align with your target audience's needs. Consider how you can solve their problems, provide value, or offer a unique selling proposition. Think about your own skills, passions, and expertise that can be leveraged to create distinctive products.

Encourage creativity and innovation during this phase.

Once you have a list of potential product ideas, it's important to validate their viability in the marketplace. Seek feedback from your target audience, either through surveys, focus groups, or online forums. Additionally, consider conducting a small-scale test launch or offering prototypes to gather valuable feedback. Make adjustments as necessary based on the insights you gain.

With validated product ideas, it's time to create a Minimum Viable Product (MVP). The MVP is a simplified version of your product that allows you to test the market and gather real-world feedback. Focus on creating a functional product that meets the core needs of your target audience while minimizing unnecessary features. This approach enables you to iterate quickly and avoid wasting resources.

Based on the feedback received from the MVP, refine and improve your product iteratively. Incorporate suggestions, address any shortcomings, and optimize your product's design, functionality, and user experience. Continuously testing and improving your product will enhance its market appeal and increase its chances of success.

In the online marketplace, effective branding and packaging are vital for attracting customers and standing out from the competition. Develop a compelling brand identity that resonates with your target audience. Design a visually appealing logo, choose an appropriate color palette, and create consistent brand messaging. Pay attention to packaging, whether physical or digital, to ensure it aligns with your product and appeals to customers.

Once your product is ready to hit the market, it's time to plan your marketing and promotion strategy. Leverage various online channels such as social media, content marketing, email campaigns, influencer partnerships, and paid advertising. Create engaging product descriptions, high-quality images or videos, and persuasive sales copy to showcase your product's value proposition.

Customer satisfaction is paramount to building a sustainable business. Provide excellent customer service by promptly responding to inquiries, resolving issues, and valuing customer feedback. Encourage customers to leave reviews, testimonials, and ratings, as positive social proof can significantly impact your sales and reputation.

Once you've established a successful product and gained traction in the online marketplace, it's time to focus on scaling and expanding your business. Here are some key steps to consider:

As your sales volume grows, optimize your operational processes to ensure efficiency and smooth order fulfillment. Consider outsourcing tasks like inventory management, shipping, and customer support to specialized service providers if necessary.

Expand your product offerings to cater to a wider range of customer needs. Use your market research and customer feedback to identify complementary products or variations of your existing product that can appeal to different segments of your target audience.

While you may have started on a specific online marketplace, explore opportunities to expand to other platforms. Research alternative marketplaces and determine if they align with your target audience and offer favorable selling conditions. This diversification can help mitigate risks and increase your reach.

Invest in building a robust online presence beyond the marketplace platform. Create a professional website or e-commerce store to establish your brand and provide a centralized hub for your products. Implement SEO strategies to improve organic visibility and consider utilizing social media and content marketing to reach a broader audience.

Seek opportunities for collaboration and partnerships with complementary brands or influencers in your niche. Collaborative marketing campaigns, cross-promotions, and endorsements can help you reach new customers and expand your brand's visibility.

Continuously monitor and analyze data related to your sales, customer behavior, and marketing efforts. Use analytics tools to gain insights into what's working and what can be improved. Make data-driven decisions and adjust your strategies accordingly to optimize your sales and profitability.

Creating and selling products on online marketplaces can be a highly profitable venture. By understanding your target audience, conducting thorough market research, and leveraging your creativity and skills, you can develop products that cater to market demand and build wealth. Remember to iterate, refine, and continuously improve your products based on customer feedback. With effective branding, marketing, and customer service, you can scale your business and expand your presence in the online marketplace. Stay adaptable, embrace new opportunities, and never stop innovating to stay ahead in this dynamic and exciting industry.

In today's digital age, selling eBooks and audio downloads online has become a popular and accessible way to share knowledge and creative content while generating income. In this chapter, we'll explore the steps you need to follow to create and sell eBooks and audio downloads successfully. From content creation and formatting to distribution and marketing, you'll learn how to leverage digital platforms to reach a wide audience and monetize your valuable creations.

Determine Your Niche and Target Audience:

Before diving into eBook and audio download creation, it's essential to define your niche and identify your target audience. Determine the topics, genres, or themes that align with your expertise, passion, and market demand. Research your target audience's preferences, demographics, and interests to tailor your content and marketing efforts effectively.

Create Compelling and Valuable Content:

Your content is the heart of your eBook or audio download. Focus on creating high-quality, engaging, and valuable content that meets your audience's needs and expectations. Develop a clear structure, organize your thoughts, and ensure your content is well-researched and accurate. Incorporate your unique insights, expertise, and storytelling skills to captivate your audience.

Format and Design:

Formatting and design play a crucial role in enhancing the visual appeal and readability of your eBook or audio download. For eBooks, convert your content into a compatible digital format such as PDF, EPUB, or MOBI. Pay attention to font styles, sizes, spacing, and page layout to ensure a seamless reading experience. For audio downloads, ensure high audio quality and consider using professional recording equipment or studios for optimal sound production.

Cover Design:

A captivating cover design is essential for attracting potential customers. Create a visually appealing and professional cover that accurately represents the content and genre of your eBook or audio download. Invest in high-quality graphics or consider hiring a professional designer to help you create an eye-catching cover that stands out in online marketplaces.

Choose Distribution Platforms:

To reach a wide audience and maximize your sales potential, select the appropriate distribution platforms for your eBooks and audio downloads. Consider popular marketplaces like Amazon Kindle Direct Publishing (KDP), Apple Books, Google Play Books, and Smashwords for eBooks. For audio downloads, platforms like Audible, iTunes, and ACX are ideal choices. Research each platform's terms, royalty rates, and reach to make informed decisions.

Publish and Set Pricing:

Follow the guidelines and requirements of your chosen distribution platforms to publish your eBooks and audio downloads. Set competitive and attractive pricing based on market research, considering factors such as content length, genre, and perceived value. Experiment with promotional pricing, discounts, and bundling options to attract new customers and drive sales.

Marketing and Promotion:

Effective marketing and promotion are crucial for generating awareness and driving sales for your eBooks and audio downloads. Implement a multi-channel marketing strategy that includes:

Creating a professional author website or landing page to showcase your work and engage with readers.

Leveraging social media platforms to build an online presence, share content snippets, and engage with your target audience.

Creating and selling eBooks and audio downloads online provides an excellent opportunity to share your knowledge, stories, and expertise while generating income. By focusing on valuable content creation, effective formatting, strategic distribution, and targeted marketing, you can reach a wide audience and maximize your sales potential. Stay dedicated, engage with your readers and listeners, and continually improve your craft to build a successful and sustainable online business. Remember, the key to success lies in delivering exceptional content and continuously adapting to the ever-changing digital landscape.

Claiming Ownership

In a world driven by ideas and innovation, the concept of ownership holds tremendous significance. Your creative property, whether it's a piece of art, a literary work, a musical composition, or even an invention, represents a part of you, your unique perspective, and your talent. Understanding the importance of owning and protecting your creative endeavors is crucial, not just for your personal growth and fulfillment, but also for the overall progress of society.

When you create something, you breathe life into a concept, a vision that originated in your mind. Your creative property becomes an extension of yourself, a manifestation of your thoughts, emotions, and experiences. It carries your personal imprint and reflects your identity as a creative individual. By embracing ownership, you are acknowledging and honoring the value of your own imagination.

Ownership grants you certain legal rights and protections. It establishes your control over how your work is used, distributed, and monetized. By registering your creative property, whether it's through copyright, patents, trademarks, or other intellectual property mechanisms, you secure exclusive rights, preventing others from exploiting your ideas without your consent. This protection ensures that you have the final say in how your work is shared and utilized, safeguarding both your artistic integrity and potential financial benefits.

When you own your creative property, you have the opportunity to establish a name for yourself in your chosen field. Your creations become a testament to your skills and expertise, positioning you as a credible and respected individual within your industry. As your body of work grows, so does your reputation, paving the way for new opportunities, collaborations, and professional growth.

Monetizing your creative property can provide you with financial stability and independence. By retaining ownership, you have the ability to license or sell your work, granting others limited rights to use it in exchange for compensation. This allows you to generate income, support yourself, and invest in future projects. Additionally, owning your creative property gives you control over licensing agreements, ensuring that your work is used in a manner that aligns with your values and vision.

Ownership of creative property is a cornerstone of innovation. When artists, inventors, and creators know that they can reap the rewards of their labor, they are motivated to push boundaries, explore new territories, and challenge existing norms. By promoting ownership, society encourages a vibrant creative ecosystem that fuels progress, inspires others, and brings forth groundbreaking ideas that can shape the future.

Your creative property represents a legacy that can outlive you. It is a contribution to the cultural fabric of society, a mark you leave behind for future generations. By owning and preserving your creative work, you ensure that your impact endures, inspiring and influencing others long after you're gone. Your creations may become a part of our collective human heritage, contributing to the evolution of art, science, and culture.

Owning your creative property is of paramount importance. It honors your individuality, protects your rights, establishes your credibility, provides economic benefits, fosters innovation, and allows you to leave a lasting legacy. Embrace your creative property with pride, and let it be a testament to your talent, passion, and unique perspective on the world.

Ownership of your creative property comes with a sense of responsibility. As the custodian of your creations, you are accountable for their proper care, preservation, and ethical use. This responsibility encourages you to engage in ongoing learning and growth, staying informed about legal and ethical considerations surrounding your creative field. By embracing responsibility, you contribute to a culture of integrity and respect for creative property, setting an example for others to follow.

When you own your creative property, you are more inclined to nurture your creative instincts and explore uncharted territories. Ownership grants you the freedom to experiment, take risks, and express yourself authentically without the fear of losing control or recognition. This environment of creative freedom fuels innovation, enabling you to push boundaries, challenge conventions, and make significant contributions to your chosen field.

Owning your creative property allows you to shape the impact your work has on the world. Whether your creations entertain, educate, inspire, or provoke thought, they have the potential to touch the lives of others. By owning your creative property, you can ensure that your work reflects your values, promotes positive change, and contributes to the betterment of society. Through your ownership, you have the power to leave a lasting and meaningful impact on individuals, communities, and even the world at large.

In embracing ownership of your creative property, you embark on a journey of self-discovery, professional growth, and artistic fulfillment. It empowers you to protect your ideas, assert your rights, and make a tangible impact on both your personal journey and the broader creative landscape. By recognizing and embracing the importance of ownership, you unlock the full potential of your creative endeavors and lay the foundation for a successful and fulfilling creative career.

If you're an author or content creator, congratulations on taking the step to share your knowledge and creativity with the world by publishing your books and teachings. Amazon, as the world's largest online marketplace for books, provides an incredible opportunity to reach a vast audience and generate monthly royalties. In this chapter, we will explore how you can effectively leverage Amazon to maximize your sales and earn consistent income from your works.

Amazon offers a platform called Kindle Direct Publishing (KDP), which enables authors and content creators to self-publish their books digitally and in print. This self-publishing process gives you complete control over your works, allowing you to set your own prices, make updates as needed, and retain ownership of your intellectual property. By self-publishing on Amazon, you open doors to a global audience and tap into their vast customer base.

When publishing your book on Amazon, pay special attention to your book description and cover. The book description serves as a sales pitch, enticing readers to choose your book over others. Make it engaging, highlight the unique aspects of your work, and clearly communicate the value readers will gain from it. Additionally, invest in a professional and eye-catching cover design that captures the essence of your book and attracts potential readers.

Setting the right price for your books is crucial for both attracting readers and generating royalties. Consider factors such as genre, length, and market demand when determining your book's price point. Pricing too high may deter potential readers, while pricing too low may undervalue your work. Experiment with different price points to find the optimal balance that attracts readers and maximizes your royalties.

Amazon offers two subscription services for readers: Kindle Unlimited and Kindle Owners' Lending Library. By enrolling your books in these programs, you open the door to additional revenue streams. Kindle Unlimited allows subscribers to read an unlimited number of books for a monthly fee, and authors receive royalties based on the number of pages read. Kindle Owners' Lending Library provides Kindle device owners with the opportunity to borrow books for free. When your book is borrowed, you receive a share of the KDP Select Global Fund.

While Amazon provides a platform for visibility, it's essential to actively promote your books to increase sales and royalties. Amazon offers promotional tools like Kindle Countdown Deals and Free Book Promotions, which allow you to offer discounts or make your book temporarily free to drive sales and gain exposure. Additionally, consider utilizing Amazon Advertising to boost visibility through targeted ads, optimizing keywords, and leveraging customer reviews to build social proof.

Beyond book sales, Amazon provides opportunities to diversify your income streams. Consider creating supplementary products or content related to your books. For example, you can offer companion workbooks, online courses, or audiobook versions of your books. By expanding your offerings, you tap into different market segments, cater to various learning preferences, and increase your overall revenue potential.

Building a loyal reader base is essential for sustained success on Amazon. Engage with your readers by responding to their reviews, comments, and messages. Cultivate relationships through author profiles, author pages, and social media channels. By connecting with your audience, you create a sense of community and foster long-term support, leading to increased book sales and word-of-mouth recommendations.

The publishing landscape, including Amazon, is ever-evolving. Stay informed about market trends, changes in algorithms, and new promotional opportunities. Continuously learn from successful authors and adapt your strategies accordingly.

As a creative individual, understanding the importance of owning your work and securing copyright protection is vital for preserving your rights, maintaining control, and ensuring the long-term value of your creative endeavors. In this chapter, we will delve into why ownership and copyright are crucial steps in safeguarding your work.

Ownership of your creative work establishes your rights as the creator. Copyright is a legal framework that grants you exclusive rights over your original works, including literary, artistic, musical, and other creative expressions. By obtaining copyright protection, you gain legal recourse against unauthorized use, reproduction, distribution, or adaptation of your work, safeguarding it from infringement and misappropriation.

Owning your work reinforces your authorship and establishes your claim as the original creator.

By asserting ownership through copyright, you secure evidence of your authorship, establishing a clear record of your creative contributions. This documentation can be invaluable in disputes or legal proceedings, ensuring that your work is attributed to you and that you receive due recognition for your artistic achievements.

Ownership of your creative work grants you control over its use, distribution, and modification. With copyright protection, you have the power to dictate how your work is utilized and who has the right to reproduce, adapt, or license it. This control ensures that your artistic integrity is preserved and that your work is presented in a manner that aligns with your vision and values.

Owning your work and securing copyright protection opens up a multitude of commercial opportunities. You have the freedom to license or sell your work to publishers, production companies, or other entities interested in utilizing your creations. By retaining ownership, you can negotiate favorable terms and royalties, enabling you to generate income from your creative pursuits and secure financial stability.

Copyright ownership acts as a shield against unauthorized use and infringement. Should someone copy, plagiarize, or exploit your work without permission, copyright protection empowers you to take legal action to enforce your rights. This deterrence factor discourages potential infringers, providing you with peace of mind and ensuring that your work remains protected and respected.

Ownership and copyright protection also serve to maintain the integrity of your creative work. By establishing your rights and ownership, you can prevent others from distorting, modifying, or misrepresenting your creations. This ensures that your work is experienced by audiences as you intended, safeguarding its artistic value and preserving its original essence.

Pace Yourself

In today's competitive business landscape, capturing and retaining customers' attention is paramount. To achieve long-term success, you need to master the art of intriguing marketing. This approach involves giving customers just enough to leave them wanting more, creating a sense of anticipation and curiosity that keeps them coming back for more. In this chapter, we will explore effective strategies to employ this enticing technique and build customer loyalty.

To effectively market to your customers, you must first understand who they are and what they desire. Conduct market research, analyze customer data, and create buyer personas to gain insights into their preferences, needs, and aspirations. This knowledge will guide you in crafting messages and offers that resonate with your target audience.

Teasers are powerful marketing tools that pique curiosity and build anticipation. Craft compelling teasers by hinting at something exciting or valuable without revealing all the details. Utilize catchy headlines, intriguing images, and engaging videos to capture attention and leave your audience craving more.

Storytelling is an age-old technique that appeals to human emotions and captures attention. Craft captivating narratives that reveal just enough to spark curiosity and create an emotional connection with your audience. Use your storytelling to create a desire for more information or experiences, leading customers to seek out your products or services.

People love exclusivity and being part of something special. Offer your customers exclusive sneak peeks of upcoming products, services, or events. Provide a glimpse into the innovation or excitement that lies ahead, but don't reveal everything. This strategy makes customers feel privileged and eager to be among the first to experience what's coming.

Limited-time offers create a sense of urgency and FOMO (fear of missing out) among your customers. Promote time-sensitive deals, discounts, or bundles that provide exceptional value. Make it clear that this offer is only available for a short period, compelling customers to take immediate action to secure the benefit. By leaving them wanting more, you create a desire for future promotions and keep them engaged.

Rather than revealing all the details about a new product or service at once, consider unveiling it in stages. This approach builds excitement and allows you to capture attention over an extended period. Release teasers, sneak peeks, and limited information over time, gradually building anticipation and leaving customers eager to discover more.

To keep customers coming back for more, engage with them through multiple channels. Utilize social media, email marketing, content creation, and interactive experiences to maintain a consistent presence and deliver enticing content. Tailor your messages for each channel while maintaining a cohesive storyline, reinforcing the desire for more information or experiences.

Create a sense of community around your brand to foster customer engagement and loyalty. Encourage customers to share their experiences, opinions, and ideas. Host contests, polls, and interactive events that allow customers to participate and contribute. This involvement will keep them invested and eagerly awaiting what's to come.

Mastering the art of intriguing marketing is a powerful way to captivate your audience and keep them coming back for more. By understanding your audience, creating compelling teasers, utilizing storytelling, offering exclusive sneak peeks, leveraging limited-time offers, unveiling in stages, engaging through multiple channels, and fostering community, you can leave customers wanting more and build long-lasting relationships. Remember, the key is to strike a delicate balance between giving enough to generate interest and holding back to maintain the allure.

Engage your audience through interactive experiences that offer a taste of what your brand has to offer. Develop interactive quizzes, games, or augmented reality experiences that provide an immersive and enjoyable way for customers to interact with your products or services. By allowing them to participate actively, you spark curiosity and encourage further exploration.

Partnering with influencers who align with your brand values can be a powerful way to generate intrigue. Work with influencers to create captivating content that showcases your offerings in an authentic and compelling manner. By leveraging their influence and reach, you can captivate their followers and entice them to seek more information about your brand.

Launch mystery campaigns that gradually reveal information or clues about an upcoming product, event, or announcement. Create a sense of mystery and intrigue by providing hints, teaser videos, or cryptic messages that spark curiosity. Encourage customers to engage with your brand, solve puzzles, or guess what's to come. The element of mystery keeps them intrigued and eager to discover the full story.

Utilize customer data and purchase history to offer personalized product recommendations or tailored content. Leverage artificial intelligence and machine learning algorithms to analyze customer behavior and provide suggestions that align with their preferences. By offering personalized recommendations, you demonstrate that you understand their needs and desires, leaving them curious about what other personalized offerings your brand might have in store.

Share behind-the-scenes content or exclusive behind-the-scenes experiences with your customers. Take them on virtual tours of your facilities, introduce them to your team, or provide glimpses into your creative process. By offering a peek into the inner workings of your brand, you create a sense of intimacy and exclusivity that ignites curiosity and leaves them wanting to be part of the journey.

Encourage customers to create and share user-generated content related to your brand. Host contests or campaigns that invite them to share their experiences, stories, or creative interpretations of your products or services. Not only does this strategy foster a sense of community, but it also generates buzz and curiosity as customers eagerly await the results and look forward to seeing their own contributions being showcased.

The internet business landscape is constantly evolving, and it's crucial to stay updated and adaptable. Dedicate time to continuous learning, whether it's through reading industry publications, attending webinars, or participating in online courses. By staying informed about emerging trends and technologies, you can make informed decisions and adapt your strategies without feeling overwhelmed by constant change.

Self-care is essential for maintaining a healthy balance in your internet business. Prioritize activities that rejuvenate your mind and body, such as exercise, meditation, hobbies, or spending time with loved ones. Taking care of yourself ensures that you have the mental and physical energy to sustain the demands of your business. Remember, a rested and rejuvenated entrepreneur is better equipped to make sound decisions and drive business growth.

Don't hesitate to seek support and collaborate with like-minded individuals in the online business community. Join relevant forums, attend networking events, and engage with peers who understand the challenges and triumphs of internet entrepreneurship. Surrounding yourself with a supportive network provides encouragement, valuable insights, and opportunities for collaboration that can help pace your growth in a meaningful way.

Pacing yourself in your internet business is not only essential for your well-being but also for the long-term success and sustainability of your venture. By setting realistic goals, prioritizing and focusing your efforts, establishing a realistic schedule, outsourcing and delegating tasks, embracing incremental growth, continuously learning and adapting, nurturing self-care practices, and seeking support and collaboration, you can maintain a healthy and manageable pace.

Remember, building a successful internet business is a marathon, not a sprint. It's crucial to find the right balance between pushing yourself to achieve your goals and taking the necessary time to rest, recharge, and reflect. By pacing yourself, you'll be better equipped to make thoughtful decisions, stay resilient in the face of challenges, and consistently deliver high-quality products or services to your customers.

Furthermore, pacing yourself allows you to maintain your passion and enthusiasm for your business in the long run. It helps you avoid burnout and enables you to enjoy the journey of building and growing your online venture.

So, take a step back, evaluate your current pace, and make the necessary adjustments to ensure that you're on a sustainable path. Embrace the power of pacing, and you'll find yourself achieving meaningful progress while maintaining your overall well-being and creating a solid foundation for your internet business to thrive.

Closing Thoughts

In today's digital age, the internet has revolutionized the way we live, work, and conduct business. It has opened up countless opportunities for individuals to create wealth and financial independence. In this chapter, we will explore various strategies and techniques that can help you leverage the power of the internet to build wealth. Whether you're looking to start an online business, invest in digital assets, or capitalize on the gig economy, the internet provides a vast array of possibilities. So let's dive in and discover how you can make wealth using the internet.

Begin by identifying your passions and interests. Research market demand and determine if there is a viable niche that aligns with your expertise and enthusiasm. Consider different online business models such as e-commerce, dropshipping, affiliate marketing, or creating and selling digital products. Evaluate the pros and cons of each model and choose the one that suits your goals.

Establish a professional website or e-commerce platform to showcase your products or services. Create engaging content and optimize your website for search engines to attract organic traffic. Leverage social media and digital marketing: Utilize social media platforms and digital marketing techniques to promote your business. Develop a comprehensive marketing strategy that includes social media campaigns, search engine optimization, email marketing, and paid advertising.

Harnessing the internet to build wealth requires a combination of strategic thinking, dedication, and adaptability. Whether you choose to create an online course, start an e-commerce business, provide coaching services, or participate in affiliate marketing, success lies in consistently providing value to your audience or customers. By leveraging the power of the internet, embracing new opportunities, and continually refining your strategies, you can tap into the vast wealth-building potential that the digital world offers. Remember, building wealth takes time and effort, so stay focused, stay motivated, and seize the opportunities that come your way.

The internet has revolutionized the way we live, work, and connect with others. It has also opened up vast opportunities for individuals to build wealth from the comfort of their own homes. In this chapter, we delve into the statistics and trends surrounding people who have successfully built wealth on the internet. We explore the diverse range of online businesses and the characteristics that contribute to their success.

The internet has democratized entrepreneurship, allowing anyone with an internet connection and a viable idea to start their own business. According to recent statistics, the number of online businesses has been steadily increasing over the years. In 2020, there were over 1.8 billion websites on the internet, and this number continues to grow. This surge in online businesses can be attributed to various factors, including technological advancements, ease of access, and a global customer base.

E-commerce has experienced tremendous growth, with more and more consumers turning to online shopping. According to eMarketer, global retail e-commerce sales amounted to $4.28 trillion in 2020 and are projected to reach $6.38 trillion by 2024. This surge in online shopping has created a fertile ground for entrepreneurs to establish successful e-commerce businesses, selling a wide range of products and services.

Affiliate marketing has emerged as a popular avenue for wealth creation on the internet. In this model, individuals earn a commission by promoting and selling products or services on behalf of others. According to a study by Statista, spending on affiliate marketing in the United States alone is projected to reach $8.2 billion by 2022. Additionally, the rise of social media platforms has given birth to the influencer economy, where individuals with a substantial following can monetize their influence by partnering with brands for sponsored content.

The demand for online education and digital products has surged in recent years. The convenience and accessibility of online learning have attracted millions of students worldwide. According to Research and Markets, the global online education market is expected to reach $319 billion by 2025. Moreover, the sale of digital products such as e-books, online courses, software, and templates has become a lucrative business model for many internet entrepreneurs.

While the internet provides opportunities for wealth creation, not everyone succeeds. Successful online entrepreneurs often possess certain characteristics that contribute to their accomplishments. Here are a few key traits:

The internet landscape is constantly evolving, requiring entrepreneurs to adapt quickly to changes in technology, consumer behavior, and market trends. Successful online entrepreneurs embrace change, continually innovate, and are agile in responding to new opportunities.

Building wealth on the internet is rarely an overnight success. It requires persistent effort, dedication, and the ability to overcome setbacks and failures. Successful entrepreneurs understand that failure is a stepping stone to success and use it as an opportunity to learn and grow.

Proficiency in utilizing technology and digital marketing strategies is crucial for online success. Successful internet entrepreneurs have a good understanding of online platforms, search engine optimization (SEO), social media marketing, content creation, and other digital marketing techniques that enable them to reach their target audience effectively.

The internet has unleashed a new era of wealth creation, empowering individuals from all walks of life to build successful businesses online. The statistics highlight the significant growth in e-commerce, affiliate marketing, online education, and digital products. However, it's important to note that success in the online world is not guaranteed. It requires a combination of factors, including a viable business idea, hard work, perseverance, and the ability to adapt to the ever-changing digital landscape.

Furthermore, it's worth mentioning that building wealth on the internet is not limited to a specific demographic. People from diverse backgrounds and age groups have found success online. According to a survey conducted by Shopify in 2020, the highest percentage of online business owners fell within the age range of 26-35, followed closely by those aged 36-45. However, individuals in their 50s and 60s also represented a significant portion of online entrepreneurs, highlighting that age is not a barrier to success in the digital world.

Moreover, the internet has opened up opportunities for individuals from different geographical locations. While certain regions, such as the United States, Europe, and Asia, have witnessed a higher concentration of successful online businesses, entrepreneurs from developing countries have also made their mark. With the internet's global reach, entrepreneurs can tap into international markets, serving customers from all corners of the world.

In terms of gender, the online business landscape has seen a notable increase in female entrepreneurs. According to a study conducted by SCORE, women-owned businesses accounted for 42% of all businesses in the United States in 2019. This trend is indicative of the inclusive nature of online entrepreneurship and the opportunities it provides for women to pursue their business aspirations.

It's important to note that while success stories of internet wealth builders often make headlines, there are also challenges and risks involved. Building a sustainable online business requires dedication, continuous learning, and the ability to navigate obstacles such as competition, changing consumer preferences, and technological advancements.

The internet has proven to be a powerful platform for wealth creation, with e-commerce, affiliate marketing, online education, and digital products paving the way for entrepreneurial success. The statistics reflect the growth and potential of online businesses, but it's essential to recognize the personal qualities and strategies that contribute to that success. By harnessing the power of the internet, individuals can build wealth and achieve financial independence, regardless of their background, age, or location.

ABOUT THE AUTHOR

Dr. Jeremy Lopez is Founder and President of Identity Network and Now Is Your Moment. Identity Network is one of the world's leading prophetic resource sites, offering books, teachings, and courses to a global audience. For more than thirty years, Dr. Lopez has been considered a pioneering voice within the field of the prophetic arts and his proven strategies for success coaching are now being implemented by various training groups and faith groups throughout the world. Dr. Lopez is the author of more than forty books, including his international bestselling books The Universe is at Your Command and Creating with Your Thoughts. Throughout his career, he has spoken prophetically into the lives of heads of business as well as heads of state. He has ministered to Governor Bob Riley of the State of Alabama, Prime Minister Benjamin Netanyahu, and Shimon Peres. Dr. Lopez continues to be a highly sought conference teacher and host, speaking on the topics of human potential and spirituality.

ADDITIONAL WORKS

Prophetic Transformation

The Universe is at Your Command: Vibrating the Creative Side of God

Creating with Your Thoughts

Creating Your Soul Map: Manifesting the Future You with a Vision Board

Creating   Your   Soul   Map: A Visionary Workbook

Abandoned to Divine Destiny

The Law of Attraction: Universal   Power of Spirit

The Gospel of Manipulation

SEERS: The Eyes of the Kingdom

PROPHETIC READINGS

What is the Holy Spirit speaking to you in this season of your life? Find out by scheduling your very own personal and private prophetic reading with Prophet Jeremy Lopez. Contact the offices of Identity Network International by visiting www.identitynetwork.net.

DREAM INTERPRETATION

What do your dreams reveal about your destiny in God? Find out through a dream interpretation session with Prophet Jeremy Lopez. Contact the offices of Identity Network International today to gain valuable prophetic insight into the world of dreams.